Cristina

Enjoy The Ride!

Bob R
2024

Rideshare by Robert
Every Ride's a Short Story

Bob Reilly

Trenton, Georgia

Print ISBN: 978-1-958877-95-1
Ebook ISBN: 979-8-88531-359-9

Published by BookLocker.com, Inc., Trenton, Georgia, U.S.A.

Names and certain details have been changed to protect the privacy of those involved.

Printed on acid-free paper.

Library of Congress Cataloging in Publication Data
Reilly, Bob
Rideshare by Robert: Every Ride's a Short Story by Bob Reilly
Library of Congress Control Number: 2022918632

BookLocker.com, Inc.
2022

This book is dedicated to the Creator God and my sweet lord, Jesus, the author, and finisher of my faith. The One whose spirit is alive and active in today's world. The One who has always been the great lover of the human family.

And, to my parents, Robert, Sr., and Gertrude, who gave life to me and my eight siblings.

The generational stories continue.

Disclaimer

I have made every attempt to provide anonymity for all individuals portrayed in this book. The names have been changed to protect the innocent, and in some cases, the not-so-innocent. I have substituted the characteristics of individuals in the stories to further my attempt to maintain anonymity. Conversations are based on my best recollection, notes, and indelible impressions. Although I have spent time with celebrities and public figures in the last seven years, I have intentionally omitted their names in this book. Locales, and other details of when and where the rides occurred, have been modified to maintain my objective of rider protection and anonymity.

Table of Contents

Forward:

What People Are Saying About the Author and the Book

This is One Ride You Won't Soon Forget

"This must-read book is all about common sense and wisdom. A solid template and path to follow on life's ride with wonderful experiences to contemplate. Bob is not only a great writer but also a good listener and the road on this ride has inspiration, creativity, joy, and honesty. You'll feel like a rideshare passenger, eavesdropping on pearls of wisdom and points of view that perhaps you hadn't considered. Bob's gifts as an accomplished humorist, author, singer, songwriter, and guitarist, allow his personable reflections and appreciation of the art of living to shine. It's essential reading. So, travel along, be a part of 'Rideshare by Robert,' swing the door open and climb in. Get empowered and entertained. This book is a gem ~ fun and important. You'll love the ride...Congratulations Robert!"

- Cerphe Colwell

Washington, DC Rock Radio broadcaster-Infinity Broadcasting/CBS Radio/Viacom/Audacy MusicPlanetRadio.com
Rock and Roll Hall of Fame Author of "Cerphe's Up, A Musical Life with Bruce Springsteen, Little Feat, Frank Zappa, Tom Waits, CSNY and Many More" Carrel Books-Skyhorse Publishing
Get a personalized-to-you hardcover copy at
https://www.jettrinkmedia.com/cerphes-indie-record-store/books

A Fascinating Peek Behind the Curtain

"Rideshare by Robert is a collection of memorable stories told with heart and humor by a true master of the craft. Hop in and let Bob Reilly regale you with tales of triumph and tragedy, humor, and warmth. Each new ride gives the reader a tantalizing glimpse into the human spirit in all its glorious, swirling madness. This book is one to keep and one to share with everyone who digs "real-life" with a humorous, poignant, artful spin."

- Susan Butler Colwell
Author of The Summerlands, Book 1 of the Angels and Elementals Series
https://susanbutlercolwell.com/

"In "Rideshare by Robert," nationally recognized Singer-Songwriter-Guitarist (and rideshare driver), Bob "Robert" Reilly, captivates his readers with tantalizing tales from his six years as a Mid-Atlantic based rideshare driver. Reilly wears many hats while transporting clients to and fro in his faithful blue Honda - sage for every age, front seat philosopher, wildcat therapist, and, at times, behind-the-wheel comedian. Providing lifts without riffs, he never wavers in his ability to embrace the various human spirits he encounters and searches for truth and meaning in the rich assortment of life experiences they offer.

Relax, fasten your seat belts, and get ready for a mesmerizing voyage into the Rideshare world of Bob Reilly."

- Mark Opsasnick, Washington, D.C.-based author, and music historian ("Rock the Potomac")

"Bob Reilly contacted me in the summer of 2010 to see if I was interested in playing eight songs with him at a coffee house in Ellicott City, Maryland. So, on September 4th, 2010, Bob and I started a musical journey that continues to this day.

His original songs are a window into the world that he sees. He uses words like a paintbrush to convey beautiful messages about life and its meaning.

Bob's "Rideshare by Robert" uses the same techniques to tell the many experiences and miles that he has witnessed. Some stories will make you think, and some will have you laughing out loud. This is one book that you won't want to put down!"

- Joe Goulait
"Reilly Goulait Band"
www.bobandjoemusic.com

"The scientific community agrees: Bob Reilly is a decidedly separate and distinct element inhabiting the Periodic Table. One of the only people on planet Earth who requires--please wait while I double-check my scientific calculations here--a grand total of zero hours of sleep. But his inherent estrangement from this activity translates into a huge win for mere mortals who otherwise pillow their heads in expectation of actual REM.

There's no reason to sugarcoat things. Bob's joie de vivre far exceeds that of the kid in the candy store. Along with basketball players who tower over seven feet, Bob's been known over the course of these rides, to drive his faithful blue Honda while simultaneously sitting in the back seat, taking careful and copious notes from clients.

Pile in, buckle up, and see where the road takes you."

- Tony Glaros
Freelance Journalist, Teacher, Writer.
www.muckrack.com/tony-glaros

"Our journey as friends began when we were just 14 years old.

Bob Reilly's talent as a singer, leader, and humorist, leaped off the stage even then, as the lead singer for a 10-piece cover band. He has impressed me again, over 50 years later, with a brilliant offering into the world of rideshare...using those same talents to transport, charm, comfort, and tell the tales of this unique community.

I have just finished and thoroughly enjoyed, reading many of the stories and the background behind the stories of his rideshare world. I am delighted and inspired that he was able to recognize God's plan for his life and work at this time. His compassion for the human soul and his gift of humor are absolute gifts to his riders and readers.

Keep up the good work Bob and keep the faith!"

- Cynthia Lynn, Ph.D.
Author of the Logan McKee Series, entrepreneur, adjunct professor, businesswoman, and world-class Nana

"Bob Reilly has blended joy, sadness, and poignancy in compelling stories. A fulfilling read!"

- Ev Foster
Author of *A Killing in Cumberland*

"My friend, Bob Reilly, and I go way back to early 1986 when our wives worked together in a restaurant. I was a DJ there on the few nights I wasn't on stage with various bands I performed with. Bob would drift over and chat with me while I spun records (yes, vinyl LPs in those days).

Bob is a versatile and highly intelligent friend who surprised me when he presented samples of his book "Rideshare by Robert" for me to peruse. Who knew Author was on his list of achievements? His writing is moving, witty, and insightful. I enjoyed reading about his experiences and anticipate more enjoyment when I finally get to read the whole book.

Keep up the good work Bob!"

- Johnny Castle
Singer-Songwriter, Musician, Teacher
Current Band: The Thrillbillys Band

Former Bands: Crank, The Nighthawks, Tex Rubinowitz & The Bad Boys, Switchblade, Bill Kirchen & Too Much Fun

"You've gotta read this book by one of the best storytellers ever. I've sat and reveled in Bob's stories for years, and I'm glad he put them together in a book that keeps you riveted from beginning to end. It's like you're there in the car while he takes on his next interesting passenger. Every ride is a short story indeed. Bob's rides throughout the Covid pandemic are particularly enamoring. He shares the different views of his customers, their conversations, and Bob's reactions to the ride experience. He puts his humor, faith, and humanity on display for all of them.

This is entertainment at its best. Bob Reilly has taken the ridesharing experience to the next level.

It's enjoyable, personable, thoughtful, and chock full of interesting folks he's met along the way."

- Paul Goldbeck
Photographer/Videographer
AU Beck Productions
240.893.7585
aubeckproductions@gmail.com
www.aubeck.com

"When Robert "Bob" Reilly was exiting the shipping and logistics industry as a "top of his field" senior executive and consultant, he was faced with a serious decision. In typical Bob Reilly fashion of turning lemons into lemonade, he quickly assessed the situation and jumped into the brave new world of rideshare, never looking back. Many other middle-aged men saw rideshare as an opportunity to make a quick buck in a changing economy, as they moved towards retirement or another career. But Bob saw a way to combine several of his passions, including his deep personal faith, his love of humanity, and his deep study of its spirit. He has creatively mixed in his own music in the process.

This book is the culmination of his original vision. I believe he would agree that so much more has unfolded because of stepping into this unique universe. This journey has opened so many possibilities and eclipsed his original goal of journaling the rideshare experience. It's rife with Bob's unique insight and humor. It solidifies his reputation as a talented storyteller. The stories range from the everyday mundane, the extraordinary, the touching, the tragic, and the all too human.

So, reach for the car door, step in, and don't forget to bring your open mind and open heart with you. You'll be greeted by a big smile and warm welcome. More importantly, you are sure to learn something new about the richness of your world, as expressed through its inhabitants.

Enjoy the "Ride" (forgive the mixed metaphor), and take a long, sweet, cool sip of this unique concoction, courtesy of Bob's 4-wheeled Lemonade Stand!

2 x Inductee Maryland Entertainment Hall of Fame
FERVOR Records Artist
410.953.0097
www.stevenroschmedia.com
www.stevenroschmusic.com
www.janglebachs.com

"In reading story after story in Bob "Robert" Reilly's collection of essays "Rideshare by Robert" it's obvious that Bob is a gifted writer and storyteller whose stories are told in an easy, conversational style. Accumulated from over 25,000 rides, many of which took place in the Washington-Baltimore region, at the height of the COVID crisis, it also becomes obvious that Bob is a man of faith with a heart of gold that he readily shares with his riders. What follows are many compassionately told stories that are sometimes humorous, sometimes heart-wrenching, sometimes thought-provoking, but always entertaining."

- Art Allen
Freelance Artist
www.graphixartdesign.com

"Join my longtime friend Bob (Robert) Reilly while he spins tales of his adventures as a rideshare driver. Clearly, riding with Bob is an experience far more profound than simply getting transported from pickup location to destination. Along the way, from Point A to Point B, riders (and readers) should be prepared to reflect, laugh, philosophize, and share deep personal connections. Bob looks beneath the surface to find commonality and humanity among his diverse cast of riders. With humor, insight, spirituality, compassion, and great tenderness, Bob takes us all on a journey through his rideshare experiences in this series of real-life vignettes and reflections.

How fortunate that we get to tag along for the ride!"

- Ellen Berrahmoun
Flutist/Writer/Photographer/Arts Educator
Photography: https://fineartamerica.com/profiles/ellen-berrahmoun
Work in Print:
The Secret Life of the City: Street Portraits of Grace and Beauty
https://www.blurb.com/b/4779584-the-secret-life-of-the-city
Music: https://soundcloud.com/jazzboxmusic

"Humorist and man of faith, Bob "Robert" Reilly, gives us a candid and refreshingly realistic view of the stories of all of us who are trying to make sense of the difficult world and lives we find ourselves in. Robert's welcoming grace he offers others in the backseat of his ridesharing Honda Civic opens the door for his passengers to share the truth of their lives in the safety of his sanctuary on wheels.

This book is filled with the grit of this life met by the faith of this storyteller saint whose journey through triumph and failure reveals itself in the empathy extended to one and all in the backseat of his little sanctuary.

Giving hope as a child of God should: one life at a time."

- Jon Paul
Writer, Consultant

Introduction

Welcome to Rideshare by Robert, and the amazing world that's known as rideshare.

My name is Bob Reilly AKA The Roads Scholar.

This book was written to capture some of the profound experiences of my last seven years as a rideshare driver. Before, during, and after the Covid-19 Global Pandemic. During this time, I completed over 25,000 rides and spent personal time with approximately 33,000 people. Most of the rides and related stories took place in the Mid-Atlantic region of the United States.

My book is broken down into journalistic short-story essays. The idea of this format was inspired by the title of the book, "Every Ride's A Short Story." This concept came to me after four months of driving. The diverse range of stories, insights, reflections, and revelations were all birthed from this basic premise.

Every ride is not a "Sunny Day Moment," nor is every observation or commentary on the rideshare experience. There's something here to challenge, offend, inspire, motivate, celebrate, reject, embrace, accept, or dismiss, for every reader.

Perhaps you'll even be entertained along the way.

If I accomplished any of the above in evoking, or in some cases, provoking, something in the reader, I believe I've accomplished something as a writer.

My heart desires that whatever these stories, perspectives, and meanderings stir in you, please take a moment to pause and listen. Perhaps through internal processing, you will gain new insight about yourself, why you think the way you do, and who you are as a person connected to this greater thing that we call humanity.

Every squeaky-clean feel-good, funny, or tearful reflection has a gritty, messy, smelly, real moment around the corner.

Welcome to the rideshare life. Welcome to my universe.

As I tell people often, this book is not for everyone, any more than being a rideshare driver is for everyone, however, this book is about everyone.

This book is about you and me. It's our story.

In fact, it's the story of humankind. Each one of us is the story.

When people tell me they would like to write a story or a book, but they don't know where to begin, I tell them, "You are the story. You are the book. Start writing."

I did not start my rideshare journey fully open to the creative process of photography and writing stories. Prior to jumping into the gig economy, I was in the middle of a six-month process of trying to reenter the job market. After 35 years in my industry, as a senior-level executive and consultant, I found myself on the outside looking in. My full-time job search, punctuated by second and third-round interviews, was an exercise in total frustration. In some cases, finding out the job I was interviewing for was given to a younger person whom I had mentored along the way. I was delighted for these people who secured a job, and at the same time, I was managing the mixed emotions of losing the potential job I was pursuing.

During all this chaos and transition, my wife lost her job. She was suffering from severe medical conditions requiring immediate attention.

I could sense a deep loss of confidence; frankly. I was struggling with my identity.

In faith, at my core, I knew who I was and that the current season would surely pass, however, in the hazy fog of swirling emotions, and external forces bearing down, the experience was earth-shattering.

Clarity was slipping away. Shell shock.

Truth is, we don't always think clearly when a bomb detonates.

A friend of mine strongly suggested I get out of my job search cycle and get on the road for a while as a rideshare driver. What? Drive total strangers around in my car? Are you kidding? However, he saw something I couldn't fully see at the time. He recognized my highly relational self. He knew instinctively I would dry up inside without daily human interaction.

So, with much resistance, I entered the world of rideshare.

For close to four months, I was very discontent. I was looking up and crying out. Trying to make sense of this new reality. I was not a very happy camper. I was processing this new life condition, questioning why, and not managing it very well. Then, one day, a bright light revelation moment filled the interior of my vehicle and overtook me.

Bam!

I was moved from "grumbling to humbling." I was exactly where I was meant to be for a greater purpose. I did not fully grasp the purpose, or how things would unfold, but I knew it in my deepest being.

In the coming months and years, I journaled four binders of stories. Stories about my personal transformation, rider stories, and stories about other rideshare drivers. I also began taking pictures and marrying them with text on Instagram and other social media.

Photojournalism.

I conceived the brand name Rideshare by Robert to umbrella this world I was entering.

A new beginning. A fresh perspective.

The creative energy was uncontainable. My heart and my senses were open. The creative vision was unfolding before my very eyes. Every conversation. Every moment of silence. Every look. Everywhere.

Creation. Transformation.

And so, with that historical backdrop, climb in, buckle up, and get ready for a wild and wonderful ride.

A ride unlike any other. Filled with unique stories about you and me.

Humanity. Many tribes and many nations.

I've arrived, I'm here. I'm ready. I see your smile, so let's get going.

You are now entering the world of Rideshare by Robert.

A place where anything can happen and usually does.

Angels of Mercy

Here is a short essay written during the Covid-19 Pandemic in 2020.

A story about the divine, and perfectly timed, appointments.

***

In life, there are seasons in which people come and people go.

Like threads in some divine tapestry.

Some seasons are lifelong, and some are 15-minute rides.

I am thankful for spending time with so many Angels of Mercy on my life journey.

The people who suddenly show up in the deepest times of need and uncertainty. The ones who provide life-giving water to a thirsty soul. These precious spirits collide with desperation and somehow shatter the deadly grip of despair through their very presence.

The sacred bearers of the essence of life.

The encouragers. The cheerleaders. The affirmers.

God's gift to humankind.

I cannot count the number of rides with people who appear to be strangers and are angels in disguise. Appointed times. I was especially blessed during the darkest days of the Covid-19 Global Pandemic. These Angels of Mercy were appearing in abundance. So many of the ride experiences were mutually encouraging.

Prayers, singing, crying, sharing raw emotions, and all the doubts and fears that plagued us during the dark hours of the pandemic. An unprecedented period in history where the driver and rider became one.

A deeper recognition of One Common Humanity. A greater realization of our temporal frailty as a species.

Outside the vehicle, chaos reigned. It seemed like death, hate and fire were consuming the globe.

Total insanity.

Humans globally at their best, and their worst. Lost and fearful. Angry and desperate.

Yet, mercy, peace, bonding, and revelation were occurring inside the vehicular sanctuary.

And precious time was being spent with an abundance of angels.

A healing balm in a sick, wounded, and hurting world.

The Human GPS (THGPS)

I would like to introduce you to a unique and interesting rider.

The Human GPS.

Almost daily, riders will ask you to revise the routing to their destination contrary to what the navigation system, otherwise known as the GPS, indicates as the best route.

As a rule, there is actually very little significant change in the Estimated Time of Arrival (ETA) on most of these rider-driven changes. Usually no more than 1-3 minutes on average.

However, approximately one-in-every 1,000th ride, you will be unforgettably greeted by The Human GPS.

These high-control creatures quickly (and quite efficiently I might add) slip into your vehicle and before you can even say hello, the conversation goes something like this:

THGPS: "Turn off your GPS! "

Me: "Okay. We will go with your route preference. I'm turning off the GPS per your request. Which way should we go?"

THGPS: "Head up Main Street for three blocks. Make an immediate left turn right past the hardware store. Drive about ½ mile and when you see flashing lights slow down. Go through the flashing lights and stay alert. You will come up suddenly on a fork in the road. This time of day you may see an elderly woman walking her two Shih Tzu dogs on the right side of the street before you reach the fork. If not, look for a bright yellow house, with a green awning, on the left side of the street. The next turn is five houses past the yellow house. Go right at the fork in the road, then make a sharp left turn on Striker Lane. Stay on Striker for eight blocks and turn right on Georgia Ave. Stay on Georgia Ave. for approximately six minutes and you will see the signs for 495. Take the West exit towards Virginia. It's a sharp turn so keep your eyes open!

Are you listening to my directions? Got it so far? "

Typically, at this point, the person is just physically entering the car, preparing to close the door, and reaching for their seat belt.

Me: "Yes, of course, I'm listening. However, I'm a little slow this early in the morning. My coffee isn't kicking in. So, can you please direct me, block by block, as we're heading toward your destination? "

THGPS: (A big, exasperated sigh), "I suppose so. Come on, let's get moving! "

I've learned there is no sense in trying to explain the potential pitfalls of ignoring the navigation system, or as I like to call it, "The Eye in The Sky", to the Human GPS.

It is a one-way street, so to speak.

Their resolve is unwavering, and for a person not to comply with their steely determination is a possible set-up for a long, uncomfortable ride.

You may even be rewarded with a rider complaint to the rideshare company in the end if you're not careful.

Much better, based on hard-earned personal experience, to suffer the relatively brief experience and bow to the strong will of The Human GPS.

Ultimately, that is the right course.

Don't Judge!

There's never a shortage of special functions and events in the Baltimore-Washington, D.C. region often referred to as the DMV (District, Maryland, Virginia).

Because Washington, D.C. is the capital of the United States, and a global draw, it is a constant buzz of activity. In the surrounding areas of Annapolis, MD, Baltimore, MD Northern VA, and elsewhere you will always be able to tap into an immense variety of things to do.

Things for every lifestyle, taste, and cause.

One such event is the Annual D.C. Drag Ball.

The evening is a colorful and provocative display of the LGBTQI + Trans and Cross-Dress Community walking through Adams Morgan, Dupont Circle, and other parts of the district.

There is a party atmosphere as an array of outfits are seen across the city moving from hotels and other designated venues.

Prior to the Covid-19 Pandemic, rideshare companies offered special services where multiple separate rides could travel in the same car. These services provided an economical price option for riders. Essentially, riders would share a vehicle with other riders moving towards a particular destination. The number of separate rides, or riders, was dependent on the vehicle capacity.

During one Drag Ball evening in D.C., I had already picked up two separate riders and I was heading towards my third, and final, rider.

We pulled up to a beautiful, well-manicured stretch of red-brick row houses near Dupont Circle.

Out of one of the buildings emerged a tall man in high heels walking very gingerly down a small flight of stairs, across the street, and towards my car.

He was dressed in a tight-fitting, sequined emerald-green gown. The dress was complete with a pair of iridescent wings on the back.

As he got closer to the car, I was able to discern a small, shimmering diadem that was placed carefully on his head.

And, to fully complete the outfit, a sparkling wand was held tightly in his left hand.

As he entered the front seat, I said, "Hello (Name), welcome to Saturday night in the city."

His deep, loud, practiced response for all in the car to hear was a potential show-stopping, "Don't Judge! "

Stunned silence.

Think fast.

I've often heard it said that timing is everything in comedy. Well, I disagree.

Perfect delivery, superb set-up, and a well-timed punchline are obviously required. However, in my estimation, one of the most critical elements of comedy is the audience.

All the fine comedic skills applied will account for nothing without a receptive and comprehending audience.

Case in point:

A modern-day comedian with edgy humor, punctuated by obligatory F-Bombs, and graphic subject matter, would not fare well at a Southern Baptist Convention.

And so, in a split second, I did not have a clue of how the individual, let alone the other people in my car might react to my quip.

In my head, I thought the response was humorous enough under the circumstances, and as I'm not a severely risk-averse person, I let it fly.

My response:

"My friend. There is absolutely no judgment in this car. I forbid such behavior. Period. We all sincerely hope your job interview goes well this evening. "

The entire car broke into abrupt laughter, albeit mixed with sighs of relief.

My ice-breaker response worked like a charm.

The sound of sweet success reinforced my strong belief that laughter is such good medicine.

The remainder of the ride was a highly animated description of the drag event by our emerald-sequined friend. During the remainder of the ride, he was pointing out his friends as they were heading over to a local hotel for one of the gatherings.

"Look everyone, there's Tommy! "

"He is so clumsy in those high heels, and he looks so ridiculous with those hairy legs, but he never listens to anyone. Ugh!"

Laughter.

For a sweet, brief journey, our friend had a warm, loving audience, who he clearly appreciated.

Apparently, his magic wand worked.

He got his special wish, and the ride wasn't a drag.

Every Pig Has Its Saturday

As you'll find, most of the stories and observations in this book center on my perspective of the rideshare world, and the immensely wide variety of riders I've been honored to meet along the way.

Below I will share a story about another rideshare driver.

Although I regularly introduce myself to other rideshare drivers in between my rides, in airport waiting zones, and at stop lights and rest areas, I obtain most stories about other drivers from my clients.

I get most of my "news" from the backseat of my car. My clients. At least, news that really matters to me. Up close and personal.

Stories.

The range of people and reasons why they have chosen to jump into the gig economy with rideshare is as varied as the riders I write about.

I am always inspired by the drivers and riders I spend time with and their personal life stories.

Their stories are my writing treasures.

During one ride, I asked a seasoned rideshare person if she had any notable memories of any rideshare drivers over the years.

She paused and told me about a recent ride where she was moved to tears.

The woman was getting ready for work, grabbed her phone, and requested a rideshare pick-up. The driver was less than 5 minutes away. She hurried, ran outside, and waved down the driver as he arrived. She was happily greeted by a young Hispanic man. They immediately hit it off and she had the opportunity to practice some of her limited Spanish during their conversation. The 20-minute ride flew by quickly, punctuated by many light moments of laughter. As they got closer to her destination, the man divulged some devastating news. The previous day his family was displaced due to an apartment fire.

He, his wife, and their three children had no place to live.

The woman was stunned.

She asked him how he could be so spirited and encouraging to a total stranger amid all he was experiencing in his personal life.

He explained that in his home country there is a popular saying, "Every pig has it's Saturday."

She didn't understand and asked if he could explain.

Her driver told her that the pig lives a pretty good life. For years, the farmer feeds the pig corn and a blend of other food products known as slop. From the pigs' perspective, life is good.

As the old, pun intended saying goes, "they're living high on the hog."

Then, one day, the fat and happy pig realizes it's Saturday.

Or, if you prefer, 'Slaughter Day.'

The man went on to say that, up until the day of his apartment fire, life was good.

He and his family were healthy and happy. Things were falling into place.

Then, suddenly, his Saturday arrived.

The passenger was amazed by how the driver was coping under such extreme circumstances. It was inspiring to see how pragmatic and calm he was in accepting his fate.

He knew with certainty that life would get better again.

And that, likely, there would be another Saturday in his future.

The car pulled up to the passenger's stop. She tearfully thanked the driver and gave him a very nice tip.

I am always amazed at the creatively surprising ways people process adversity when it shows up on their doorstep. Times when the person must confront the reality that they are completely at the mercy of their circumstance and no longer in control. I often ask, "how are you getting through this situation? How are you holding up?"

Many respond that they're leaning on their faith. Still, others share a range of ways in which they process their fate.

I was moved by this driver's story, and I hope you enjoyed it as well.

For, we will all experience "Saturdays" in our lives, and a positive perspective is key.

Waiting for Jesus

Spain is a traditionally Catholic country, and historically, the use of the name Jesus is common. Hispanic culture draws on many of the Spanish traditions, including the use of the name Jesus.

In Spanish, the name is pronounced: "Hay-Soos."

In other cultures, and traditions, the use of the name is considered blasphemous.

Still, other world religions take no issue with the use of faith names like Krishna or Mohammed. During my last seven years of driving, I have met quite a few people named Mohammed and Krishna.

In Christianity, the faithful believe that their Lord, Jesus, will come again to rule through all eternity.

Or what is commonly referred to as The Second Coming.

I always have a good chuckle when I see the name Jesus pop on the rideshare app.

Could this be the day?

Could this be the one?

Then, of course, the waiting part.

This morning I pulled up to a house in suburban Maryland.

I waited outside for my rider, Jesus, who had just sent me a message that he was running late.

Another self-chuckle.

When Jesus finally appeared in front of his townhouse, he was not clothed in flowing white robes.

No, this twenty-something Jesus was in shorts, tee-shirt and running shoes.

Heavily tattooed with depictions of Jesus, the Madonna, Semper Fi, and other popping artwork.

When he got into my car, I turned around, looked at him, and said, "Greetings in the name of Jesus!"

He said hello, and he cracked up laughing.

I thought to myself, this guy seems to have a fun spirit, so let's roll!

I told him I didn't expect Jesus to be so colorfully tattooed when he returned.

We both had a good laugh.

He took time to explain the meaning behind each tattoo art on his body.

Beautiful and well-done body art.

More creatively thoughtful than a random "hey, let's get tattooed" alcohol-inspired group decision during a night of bar crawling in downtown Baltimore.

Family memories, faith, and deep, personal vows to never forget.

I showed him the less-than-impressive tattoo on the palm of my hand.

It is a faint, barely noticeable dark grey mark I received in the 4th grade.

Another student jabbed me during a sword fight with a #2 pencil.

The Mark of Zorro!

Another laugh.

The ride continued and we talked about a few different things along the way.

We finally arrived at his stop.

Big smiles and fist bumps.

Gracias Jesus, and adios!

#MoPeaceLiving

Mo (More) Peace Living.

I came up with a visual concept years ago that I want to share with you.

Over the past seven years or so, I have asked thousands of people what this means as I extend my two fingers in a peace or victory sign. Most of these interactions have occurred in my rideshare world as a humorous ice-breaker.

You can see a depiction of the three-finger sign on the book's front cover. My longtime friend, and amazing artist, Art Allen (www.graphixartdesign.com), provided the sketch. It captures the essence of so many rides and conversations with so many people.

Typically, once I show the person(s) two extended and spread apart fingers, they respond, " Oh, that's a peace sign."

I then add one more finger to the mix and ask them, "Okay, if two fingers are a peace or victory sign, what is this?"

I get a wide range of responses, but most are simply, "I don't know."

I tell them, "Well, if two fingers are peace or victory, then adding a third finger represents Mo, or More Peace or Victory!"

Usually, this revelation of met with smiles and laughter.

As it should be.

More peace. More victory.

Something our world can use an abundance of, yes?

"Mo Peace is God's Peace"

Spread Mo Peace Living!

Cultural Anthropology

When I was in college, I took several undergraduate anthropology courses.

As it turned out, I didn't "dig" the archeological anthropology.

However, I was stirred by the idea of becoming a cultural anthropologist. I was intrigued by societies and distant cultures from a very young age. The curiosity was uncontainable. I would guess my fascination began when I was around 8 years old.

Although I was never directly confronted, I believe my parents may have questioned my deep interest as a pre-teen in magazines such as National Geographic. I often wondered if they recognized my sincere and driving desire to see the beautiful photography from lands I could only imagine or if they suspected a side motivation was the ability to see topless women from various countries.

Oh well, ...

Guess I'll never know at this point, may they rest in peace. We never had that conversation. In fact, there are so many conversations I wish we had, especially as I age and the years of their departure from this earth continue to mount. In a strange, but real way, the further away I am physically from their departure, the closer I am to seeing them again.

I can honestly tell you that my imagination soared as I read stories and saw the images in the publication. My hunger to explore my curiosity further was found in books, on the movie screen, and through television broadcasts such as The Undersea World of Jaques Cousteau, Wild Kingdom, and eventually, the National Geographic TV series.

Heaven on earth!

Bottom line: I was truly captivated by an overwhelming sense of wonder and adventure in the great big world beyond my immediate universe.

As a boy, I wanted to travel and see the world. I wanted to experience, and possibly even immerse myself in the diversity of so many cultures across the globe. I felt I was on the edge of the pool of humanity and eager to dive in. This barrage of available information about other cultures from around the globe was absolutely stirring my appetite for something more.

Something bigger. Something different and mysterious. Something outside of my seemingly ordinary life growing up in the Washington D.C. suburbs. Going to school, playing sports, hanging out with family and friends, and watching the days pass.

The desire of my heart has been fulfilled throughout my adult life as I have traveled the world for both my work and pleasure. Part of this adventure included traveling to China, Korea, and The Philippines to adopt our three children, who are now all in their twenties.

Daily, my quest for deeper multi-cultural, multi-ethnic, and multi-racial experiences is now realized in my community, my church life, my friendships, my non-profit work, and my rideshare work.

As the years go by, and in retrospect, one of the greatest cultural events of a lifetime was occurring right before my eyes. And, as these things often happen in life, I believe I missed some of the wonder of the very reality I was placed in as a child. At times, too drawn by the *other*, that is, the wanderlust that was calling me, and somewhat missing the amazing life I was in.

As well, these days, popular culture tends to downplay traditional families in lieu of a broader cultural family or tribe. To include value systems that may be foreign or counter to a great many traditional families, regardless of their country of origin.

Through all the mixed cultural messaging, I can never underestimate the gift of growing up in a large family.

I am one of nine children.

My mother and father were both wonderful people and beautiful examples of a strong work ethic. Irish-Italian descent (and, as I recently discovered through DNA testing, almost 2% Guinean and Gambian), both of my parents were born in New Jersey and relocated to the Washington D.C. area after World War 11.

My father, Robert Sr., was a dedicated worker outside the home. My mother, Trudy, was the inside job. In retrospect, I think Trudy got the short end of the stick managing nine kids.

Can you imagine?

They both loved us immensely.

I have two older sisters, two younger brothers, and four younger sisters. All precious gifts and blessings in my life. All life teachers and life messengers who continue to teach me to this day.

A novel and a mini-series could be written with nothing but stories about growing up in my family and the ongoing stories as the tree blossoms with new fruit.

The great cultural adventure I almost missed.

I thank God for opening my eyes to this truth which only becomes sweeter as our family tree continues to grow and expand. I am thankful to be a branch of our family history tree. I am thankful for my ancestors, now including my newly discovered roots tied to Gambia and Guinea.

I am thankful for the beautiful treasures yet to be added to the tree, and the future they will know.

I am thankful for stories upon stories upon stories.

Thankful.

A Fishy Ride Called LaWanda

Much of my rideshare work, especially in the community non-profit universe, involves transporting people to and from various clinics, treatment centers, shelters, rehabs, and such.

The work is not for the faint of heart. And, your heart must be completely in the game, so to speak.

One ride request in Baltimore involved picking up a woman named LaWanda.

(Disclaimer Reminder: I do not use the actual names of riders, or my clients, anywhere in the book.)

As I approached the treatment center several blocks outside the Inner Harbor district, I noticed a small group of people hanging around on the street. Suddenly, a middle-aged woman ran to my car from the opposite side of the street yelling loudly "Let me in. Open the door. Blue car. Blue car."

She was wearing a long grey coat and appeared to be quite upset. She was screaming at the top of her lungs and all the people on the street turned to see what was going on.

"I'm late. Where the f*** have you been you mother- f*****?"

I asked her calmly, "Are you LaWanda? "

She yelled and pounded on the roof of my car, "Stop asking me that s*** mother- f*****!"

"Open the f****** door."

I calmly responded, "before I let you in the car, and we drive to your destination, I just need to be sure. Are you LaWanda?"

"My name is Robert. Am I the driver who is supposed to pick you up?"

Her extremely loud response was, "I know who you are b****! Stop f****** with me. Stop F****** with me or I'll report your F****** A** for harassing me! "

And so, less than half-convinced that she was LaWanda, I let her in the car to avoid further escalation.

We drove approximately one city block and she began yelling and pounding the back of my seat with her fists.

"Malik, Malik!"

"Where the f*** are you going b****?"

At first, I thought she was on her phone shouting at someone.

I pulled over and asked her if everything was okay.

She leaned up to my right ear and screamed, "Yeah, that's right Malik. I'm talking to you mother- f*****. Where the f*** are you taking me? "

I again explained to her that my name is not Malik, it was Robert.

At that point, she totally went off the deep end.

"Where's Malik? Who are you? Where are you taking me?"

"I was told to look for a Light Blue Toyota. Who are you? "

I tried to explain again, "I've told you several times, my name is Robert. This is a Dark Blue Honda. I don't know Malik. I'm sorry. I believe you're in the wrong car."

At that point, she vigorously pounded the back of my seat and shouted, "Let me out of this car mother f*****. You're making me miss my ride with Malik! "

She got out of my car, slammed the door, and was cussing to the sky. I slowly drove away and proceeded to drive back around the block to the treatment center in search of my intended rider, LaWanda.

I pulled up in front of the treatment center, and the same group of people was still hanging around outside the building.

Uh Oh!

The same animated woman who just got out of my car runs up to me asking, "Hey, are you, Malik?"

"Where the f*** have you been? "

Does anybody remember the movie Groundhog Day?

Anyway, she clearly didn't remember I was the same guy she was screaming at five minutes earlier.

I told her, "I'm not Malik. I'm sorry. Please calm down, I'm sure Malik will be here soon to pick you up. "

Thankfully, before the situation went quickly downhill, the correct rider, LaWanda, walked up to my car, identified herself, and we were on our way.

Another day, another ride, another story.

Funny how these things happen.

"Every ride's (whether it's the correct ride or not) a Short Story. "

As we drove off, and I caught a glimpse of the yelling woman receding in my review mirror, I lifted a quick prayer for her.

I hope she finally got her anticipated ride with Malik and her meds!

Second-Hand Buzz

Frankly speaking, weed, alcohol and other intoxicants are simply part of the Rideshare experience. Sometimes, altered state rides occur at 2 am on a Saturday morning. Sometimes, they occur at 7 am on a Tuesday morning heading into work.

It's just a matter of mathematics. Percentages.

Either way, it's part of the gig.

I will tell you firsthand that there is one loose calculation to consider if you're thinking about becoming a rideshare driver. Or, if you decide to become a driver, to help determine what is your tolerance for crazy and when you decide to hit the road.

1. Weekend nights increase the intake of a wide variety of substances, and a wide variety of substances will typically increase the "Drama Factor."
2. If you seek drama, and a higher count of wild stories, accidents, and the possibility of an array of human secretions, including the occasional hurl in the back seat of your car, then drive late-night weekends. Go ahead and get your fill of drama. There's plenty out there.
3. Guaranteed exponential increase in riders losing things in your vehicle

I would suggest always keeping barf bags in your vehicle just in case.

So, in my case, after years of late-night, early morning hours weekend driving, I decided to back off a bit. As a rule, when the sun goes down, I head home, or I may head off somewhere to perform live music in the region.

In retrospect, I did have some great rides during those weekend "party time" driving experiences. Lots of fun rides. Lots of wild rides. Lots of unpredictable conversations.

Lots of interesting stories, for sure.

However, it also involved some nasty and dangerous stuff.

Spilled drinks, vomit, people falling asleep in my car, creepy dark alley pick-ups and drops in the city, drug deals, weapons, lost items, obnoxious behavior, people commandeering the music with their low-end pounding playlist at peak volume until the windows in the city were close to shattering, wrong riders hopping in my car and refusing to get out, sexual escapades in the backseat, sexual overtures by riders, argumentative people, flashers, bloody fights in the car, and more.

Even two marriage proposals!

The Drama Factor.

One evening I picked up a person who was outside a bar adjacent to a metro station in town. He was totally wasted and circling planet Mars for a messy landing. The person slowly, and erratically, inched towards my vehicle.

I was thinking to myself, "well, this should be interesting."

In these situations, I exercise grace until I determine if this is a medical condition or a medicated condition.

Or both.

It didn't take long to find out.

The rider approached, opened the rear passenger door, and stood outside the car for around two minutes.

I waited.

I then heard a very distinct sucking sound as the person was taking the last big hit of whatever he was smoking. He got into the car. He was so disoriented that he exhaled heavily after he closed the rear door. A cloud of thick smoke filled the car. I laughed, rolled down the windows, opened the sunroof, and asked him in a cheerful voice, "Hey man, are you okay?"

He grunted and quickly nodded out in the back seat.

Bingo!

I was inspired to write both a story and, eventually, a song.

The lyrics to my original Rideshare Song, Second-Hand Buzz, are below.

Second-Hand Buzz by Bob Reilly

You needed a ride, so I picked you up
Right outside the bar
You took your last hit when you opened the door
Then you exhaled in my car

I got a Second-Hand Buzz
I got a Second-Hand Buzz
It ain't no lie
Believe me cuz
I got a Second-Hand Buzz
I knew you were wasted when I pulled up
I mean, you could barely stand
My thoughts were confirmed when you leaned up and asked me
"When will this plane land? "

I got a Second-Hand Buzz
I got a Second-Hand Buzz
It ain't no lie
Believe me cuz
I got a Second-Hand Buzz

You were mumbling something from the back seat
I could hardly tell
I've got to admit, I was taken aback
When you began to yell

You said,
"When they say no, we get high
When they say yo we get high
When they go low, we get high
But I really don't know why"

My, My, My

After a while, I started seeing things
I was feeling kind of silly
I looked at your face, and it kept on changing
From Snoop Dog back to Willy

I got a Second-Hand Buzz
I got a Second-Hand Buzz

It ain't no lie
Believe me cuz
I got a Second-Hand Buzz

This song, and several other originals, have been written with lyrics and music. They are being recorded for an album of songs inspired by stories from the Rideshare by Robert book and the rideshare experience in general. The songs will be available on all your popular music streaming platforms.

Rideshare By Robert: The Music

A Father's Day Reflection

Last week on a ride in the Maryland suburbs, I had a deep and honest conversation with an elderly Black woman. During our 30-minute drive, she disclosed how weary she has become over all the hatred and violence in our world today.

We wasted no time. We went deep.

We spent a good amount of time during our ride talking about racism, social justice, God, and our families. We were openly sharing our unique perspectives. Somewhere during our conversation, I told her about my family upbringing.

I was one of nine children.

My parents taught us, at a very young age, how God created humankind in his image. We will meet people who look different from us on the outside, and in God's eyes, we are all part of his colorful creation.

God does not see the outer person. God sees the heart. My parents would use nature, animals, plants, and flowers to illustrate the beauty in God's creative diversity.

Perfect Creator God. Beautiful, imperfect human creation.

The rest is history unfolding.

There are quite a few riders who enjoy engaging in open conversation about the times we live in, and usually, it doesn't take long before the subject of race enters the conversation.

Frankly, I'm glad it does.

Let's get on with things people!

So, during the conversation with the woman, I shared some relevant personal history which helped to put some skin on the bones of our conversation.

My father, Robert Reilly, Sr., was a District Sales Manager for General Mills, the U.S.-based food company. In the early 1960s, one day my father came home with a person he just hired onto his team. A Black man by the name of Will. My siblings and I immediately fell in love with Will. We could see his kind and humorous heart. He loved to laugh, and he loved being with us. For us, that was all that mattered.

We always looked forward to Will's visits.

A few years later, my father was offered a nice promotion with General Mills. The only catch was that he had to relocate to Minneapolis, MN. We were living in Maryland at the time and my father declined the promotion. He didn't want to disrupt our family by pulling the kids out of school. Once my father made his decision to decline the offer, he actively advocated to get his friend, Will, the promotion.

At this point in my story, the woman rider began to cry. She said, " Your Dad was a pioneer. "

Her comment was profound.

The emotion in her words made me cry also because I never processed his life, and this particular action, as anything extraordinary. It was just who he was. However, when I look at the extreme divisiveness, hate, anger, and demonization of people in our country, and across the globe, based on skin color, I am so proud of my father. I'm eternally thankful for his many life lessons.

I do not believe you are born a hateful racist. I believe it's taught. And, by the way, all people have the potential to be racists. No one race has full ownership. Human history has clearly taught us that lesson.

Judging people on their melanin count, and shades of skin tone may be one of humankind's saddest realities.

Imagine the rose hating the lily. Go figure.

At its root, racism is *heart disease*, and anybody can become sickened by this ravaging killer. Tend the garden of your heart carefully. Kill the weeds of racism, hate, and blame before they take over a thing of beauty. Life is too short and too precious to waste on such things.

I love you and miss you dearly Robert Sr.

Thank you, and Happy Father's Day.

Great Big World

A few years back I wrote a song inspired by the fascination of how much there is to see, learn, and appreciate on our earthy pilgrimage. Struck by how little time we're given to grasp the fullness of it all. King Soloman, who unabashedly tasted life to the fullest, summarized our earthly pursuits as pure vanity. He was King David's son and authored the book of Ecclesiastes. Soloman had a reputation as a very wise person. The summary that everything we do under the sun in our lifetime is pure vanity may be true. Still, our curiosity, wonder of life, love of people, and thirst for knowledge and meaning, will continue to drive us onward. Perhaps Soloman was experiencing the "crash of excess" and going through a depressed period in his life when he penned these thoughts. Not sure, but we are fully aware of the emptiness that often enters the human soul when a person "arrives" and begins to struggle with the searing question, is this it?

My song below summarizes the inability of a person to completely experience everything in this world as a pursuit too great, bigger than you can see, or wrap your mind, or resources around. And, to see is to know on one level. For a person to fully realize the breadth and scope of this world's minute detail is impossible. Seeing is also imperfect due to our information filtering. We are imperfect; therefore, our seeing is imperfect. This helps explain why ten people seeing the same thing will each have a different response if asked, "what did you just see?"

How much of the truth, or reality of something do we simply miss, or misinterpret?

I would venture to say a lot.

I have often described my rideshare experience with so many people from many walks of life and diverse backgrounds as a painter's palette full of rich colors. So many blends from which to choose.

In this book, in stories like Cultural Anthropology, I share my heart's desire as a young child to experience many cultures first-hand. Many tribes, and many nations as part of my life journey. I am thankful for what I've seen and experienced thus far, including the amazing opportunities in the rideshare world, to paint so many pictures with my overflowing palette of many hues.

Lastly, the spinning wheel line in the song is descriptive on many levels. On a deeper level, spending time on the spinning wheel refers to life, the universe, and the passage of time. To some extent, the idea of us being part of the many spinning wheels in the "machinery" of our daily existence.

The obvious allusion to the spinning wheel is the wheel on my vehicle.

John Lennon's song, "Watching the Wheels," supposedly referenced thousands of wheels of vehicles each day, going round and round, marking the passage of time and life in New York City.

When I wrote the line in the song, both images, life, and car tires, popped into my mind.

In the end, the song is an expression of celebration for this life, for this world, its people, and its great vastness.

Great Big World by Bob Reilly

It's a Great Big World
Bigger than you can see
It's a Great Big World

It's a Great Big World
With new realities
It's a Great Big World

Some people walk around like they know it all, uh-huh
But we're just a tiny speck on a spinning ball in space
In the blink of an eye, our time is done, and heaven knows the rest
Just passing through what we call this human race

It's a Great Big World
Bigger than you can see
It's a Great Big World

It's a Great Big World
With new realities

It's a Great Big World

I had a little time on the spinning wheel, uh-huh
But it's just another field that the locust ate away
In the blink of an eye, the hope's restored, and heaven knows the rest
Just overjoyed we can know a better way

It's a Great Big World
Bigger than you can see
It's a Great Big World

It's a Great Big World
With new realities
It's a Great Big World

Every tribe in every nation
Sing a song of celebration
Every boy and every girl
Sing along, It's A Great Big World

This song, and several other originals, have been written with lyrics and music. They are being recorded for an album of songs inspired by stories from the Rideshare by Robert book and the rideshare experience in general. The songs will be available on all your popular music streaming platforms.

You can now listen to an earlier version of Great Big World on your favorite music streaming platform.

The song was originally released on my latest album, Bob Reilly, Work in Progress.

I hope you enjoy the music!

Limping Louise

This morning I picked up a woman who was leaving her home just as the sun was rising over the city. I noticed she was walking with a limp.

Immediately, the Old Testament, or if you prefer, the Hebrew Bible story of Jacob raced across my mind.

In the book of Genesis, the account details how Jacob wrestled with God.

Some interpret the account as a spiritual wrestling match, and others believe that it was a physical wrestling match. Some believe it was not God with whom Jacob wrestled, but rather an angel, or another heavenly representative.

As for me, I understand first-hand about spiritually wrestling with God. It's been a part of my life journey. So, I will go with the God mud pit scenario on a spiritual level.

I've never had a physical wrestling match with God, although I would argue the intensity of some of my matches could be considered physical.

I'm certain other strong-willed, hard-headed people can also relate to this subject.

My point is that Jacob eventually lost the wrestling match with God.

And Jacob walked away with a limp.

I am inexhaustibly curious about many things. Also, I am driven in my pursuit of stories. My precious gems.

How did this woman receive her limp?

A story waiting to unfold, and my journalistic salivary glands were beginning to pump uncontrollably. As well, I needed to accomplish my mission within 12 minutes.

Strategy:

1. Build a Quick Relationship.
2. Create A Safe Environment So She Could Share Her Story.
3. Be Transparent About My Own Story.

A quick prayer and.........

Entry Point.

Me: "We've been given a beautiful sunrise this morning Louise."

Louise: "Oh yes. I am so grateful for another day."

Me: "Me too. You know, I have been so blessed over the past six years. My driving has allowed me to witness more sunrises and sunsets than I've ever seen in my entire life. Plus, I've been able to share the marvelous wonder with other people. A common experience with other humans. I am so thankful for this gift. Louise, the amazing thing is there is no guarantee that the sun is going to rise. I believe many people go about life assuming the sun will rise, and, at the end of the day, set. I often imagine how different the world would be if the sun did not rise. How all the priorities across humanity would instantly shift. We caught a glimpse of this reality in the deepest, darkest days of the Covid-19 Global Pandemic. I had my own personal earth-shattering event when I found myself paralyzed from the neck down at the age of 52. My life instantly changed. My priorities instantly shifted. The world, as I knew it, ended."

Louise: "Oh my God. I completely understand what you're saying. How did it happen? How were you paralyzed?"

Me: "I got a very rare condition called Guillain-Barre Syndrome. It's an autoimmune malady. Essentially, your immune system attacks the peripheral nerves in your body. In my case, I was paralyzed from the neck down, and eventually had to learn to walk again."

Louise: "You know, 15 years ago, I and two friends crossed the street to go shopping. A drunk driver ran a red light and hit all of us. My two friends died instantly at the accident scene. I was in a coma for over a month. I've had 16 surgeries. But, by God's mercy, I am still alive and walking."

Me: "Amen Louise! God most definitely had a great purpose for keeping you here on earth. I can tell you personally that your story, and everything you have gone through, have deeply inspired me this morning. More than ever, I am certain this morning's sunrise was meant for both of us."

Louise: "Yes indeed! Amen!

We pulled up to her place of work, and as Louise got out of my car she said, "Thank you and God bless you,"

"Same to you Louise. Have a blessed day."

Well, as she limped slowly away from my car, I not only got my story, but something far greater than words could ever express.

My hope is for another sunrise.

Roads Scholar Tip

Practical Preparation for an Awesome Ride

I hope you find this information helpful in ensuring your ridesharing is a safe and enjoyable experience. Both the driver and rider can benefit from this information, and I have learned much along the way. Seven years and over 25,000 rides later, I'm pleased to pass along some helpful tips.

Preparation is not only practical but also purposeful.

Some of the practical elements for the driver include:

1. Maintain your vehicle properly. Try to stay on a vehicle maintenance schedule.
2. Wash and vacuum the vehicle regularly and periodically have the car detailed.
3. Odor eaters or a light fragrance can help the interior smell fresh.
4. Gas up.
5. The rideshare app will also prompt the drivers before logging in. This could include highlighting certain driving policies in effect. For example, wear a mask, roll the windows down, etc.
6. Make sure the app is plugged in, working, and connecting to the navigation app.
7. Make certain the amp (rideshare light) is plugged in and is lit on the dashboard.
8. Be sure the rideshare platform logo is in the passenger side window.
9. When you accept a ride and arrive at the pick-up location, you will be given a wait time, usually, 5-minutes, for the passenger to arrive. Once the time has expired, attempt to call the rider before you cancel the ride and move on. I typically wait another 30-60 seconds after the call in the event the rider is stuck in an elevator or rushing out the door.

Here are some practical rider preparation tips:

1. Make sure that you check your rideshare app to ensure it's working properly.

2. Double-check that you've entered both the pick-up location and drop-off locations correctly. Take a close look at the location addresses before you activate the ride request. Sometimes the wrong location is selected from the drop-down options, and this can result in sending the driver to the wrong location. A costly mistake both in time and money.
3. Add any notes on the ride. For example, "I'm in the green building next to the medical center." "You're picking up my mother. She will be out front with a walker." "Please call when you arrive." "I have a yellow jacket on, and I'll be waving my phone."
4. Be ready to roll when the driver arrives. If possible, be at the door or curbside.
5. Once the driver's wait time expires, usually around 5 minutes, they're supposed to attempt to contact the rider before canceling the ride. Suggestion. If you are running behind, reach out to the driver and explain your situation before the wait time runs out.
6. If you find your pick-up address causes problems with the GPS, for example, the driver always drives to the back of the building to pick you up, then try this trick. Put the address of the building across the street or adjacent to you in the rideshare app. Oftentimes, this tricks the GPS and corrects the problem. The driver will be looking for someone to leave the building across the street, but you will see the car arrive out front. A quick and simple solution to the problem.

   Trust me, these little particulars can make a big difference in setting the stage for an excellent rideshare experience.

   So, be safe, and enjoy the ride!

The Echo People

There is a unique animal that shows up several times a week in my rideshare world.

The Echo Person.

Unlike The Human GPS story which I shared in this book, the echo people don't tend to give you a detailed breakdown of the route to their destination before they fasten their seat belts. Nor do they insist you turn off the GPS so they can direct the route.

Oh no, the echo types will simply repeat everything the GPS indicates on the route.

I use an audible voice GPS which reinforces the visual routing. I find this tool very helpful.

When I'm approaching a traffic light and I'm supposed to turn right, the GPS "voice" firmly tells me to, "turn right in a quarter-mile."

Within 2 seconds, from my back seat, the echo person yells, "turn right at the light in a quarter-mile."

I used to take a pause and consider the person may have a hearing problem. So, I would turn up the volume on the GPS.

Nope.

Not a hearing problem, at least in most cases.

Possibly a control issue, or something else, but not a hearing problem.

GPS voice says, "turn left on North Capitol Street."

Echo Person blurts out, "make a left turn up ahead on North Capitol."

I just smile and make a left turn.

Being a naturally curious person, especially when it comes to human behavior, I inquired with a few echo people why they "do the echo thing."

I'm always half-expecting someone to respond to my query with a "why do you do the echo thing?"

In most cases, the response has been that they either wish to be helpful or reinforce the directions in the event I didn't hear the GPS. Some admitted that it was purely self-talk to calm them down during the ride.

Okay, fair enough, but still a little over-the-top albeit humorous.

Finally, the echo I've been looking forward to during the entire ride.

App: "You have arrived," with an echo from behind me, "You have arrived."

Me: "Thanks again! Have a good day and be blessed!"

Rider: "Thanks again! Have a good day and be blessed!"

And, so, it goes…………

Accidents Will Happen

The following essay was originally written in the early days of the Covid-19 Global Pandemic. It was part of a series of essays I wrote as a journaling exercise entitled Diary of a Hugger During the Covid-19 Crisis.

It was an amazing experience to drive during an unprecedented period in our planet's history.

On many levels, the experience changed me as a person forever.

There were many conversations, which continue to this day, about the origins of the virus which spread across our world like an out-of-control wildfire.

Embers continue to flicker.

***

On April 9th, I put out a social media message entitled Accidents Will Happen. The media post was accompanied by an Elvis Costello song by the same name.

I shared my concerns that the Covid-19 outbreak possibly originated from the Level 4 Biosafety lab (BSL) in Wuhan, China. The Wuhan Institute of Virology.

One of two Biosafety labs in China.

I've continued to pursue the history of this lab since my initial message, and the lab's research on bats, wet markets, Corona, and other viruses. U.S. Intel, and members of the scientific community, have expressed their own concerns about the safety of both labs in China over the years.

Each day, I spend time with a wide range of people, from various backgrounds, countries, and professions.

A few days ago, I shared a ride with a young woman from a mainstream news outlet in Washington, D.C. She's and her team have been busy digging into the origins of the Coronavirus outbreak in Wuhan. At the time, they were primarily considering the popular wet market theory.

I pleaded with her to please not to ignore the possibility of the outbreak tied to the lab in Wuhan, and she assured me her team would include the lab as part of their investigative process.

Media outlets are now focusing on several reasons for the outbreak, including an accidental release. Some even suggest an intentional release. As of this writing, I'm more in the camp of the possibility of an accidental release. I don't yet buy into the idea of something more menacing or nefarious. Our own country has experienced accidental lab releases over the years, and I'm not convinced of any wrongful intentions in China.

I believe we're in a glass house on this subject when it comes to casting stones.

However, the fact that such lab accidents can occur here actually strengthens the possibility of accidental lab releases elsewhere.

Human error.

Over the past week, I've heard multiple reporters pressing President Trump during his daily Covid-19 Updates on the issue of a possible breach at the Wuhan Lab. There's also been print media raising the issue and making strong cases for why this may have occurred.

This is encouraging.

Thankfully, it appears as though my rider honored her promise and got the ball rolling with a handful of reporters who have begun to raise the issue.

I'm hopeful that, one day, we may uncover the truth of what happened. Globally, the many lives lost, and their grieving families, deserve nothing less than the truth.

I want to make it clear that I love my country and I love the people of China. My own daughter is from China. Regardless of where these catastrophic events occur, it would be nice for the world to know the truth. To me, truth is freedom, however difficult the truth.

Perhaps we can make global progress in pursuit of what happened. Perhaps we will never know.

So, go ahead and wear your face masks, but please don't cover your eyes and ears.

Let alone your brain, common sense, and logic.

Homeless

It was an early morning pick-up in Washington, D.C., not too far from Capitol Hill. As I approached my rider, I saw a slender, frail-looking woman holding on to a light pole. She was dressed in, what appeared to be, faded garments. A long robe with a hood. When I pulled up to let her in, it became clearer that her clothes were stained and torn. Not sure, but I speculated that she was possibly living on the street.

She gingerly moved towards my car, opened the rear door, and climbed in the back seat.

I greeted her saying, "Good morning. How are you doing?"

Other than simply getting her to her destination, I wanted to see if there was anything I could do to help, and possibly determine if she was, in fact, homeless.

In addition to my ridesharing, I work for a community non-profit. You will read more detail about my unique work in my story, Patrons for Peace Project, later in this book.

The organization does advocacy work with the homeless and underserved communities. I love the work and the mission. I am very comfortable trying to meet the needs of people, in whatever situation they're experiencing, if I'm able.

She pondered my question for a moment, and responded, "Thank You. I am not doing good. I am very sad."

I took a moment to look in my rear-view mirror.

Her elderly face had a leathery, dark brown, and heavily wrinkled appearance. I guessed she was somewhere in her 80's.

I will never forget her eyes. Piercing and soaking with tears.

I asked her, "is there anything I can do for you?"

She answered emphatically, "Yes! Pray for my country, Afghanistan."

At that point, I knew and understood.

It was abundantly clear.

She was, indeed, "Homeless."

Far from her home and hurting deeply.

The ride was only around five minutes long.

When we arrived, I did as she requested, and prayed.

She thanked me, got out of the car, and quickly disappeared into the early morning fog.

Essential Workers, Heroes, & Our Passing Fancies

This brief essay below was written during the Covid-19 Global Pandemic in 2020.

You may recall how the media and popular culture was gushing over our essential workers and healthcare heroes during the darkest days of the pandemic. Our world was turned upside down, and the planet was in shock. World governments were in chaos attempting to manage the onslaught of an unseen enemy.

People around the world were dying, getting sick, on lockdown, and living in fear.

The stage was set.

Enter a cultural flood of reverence for our essential workers and heroes.

For many months, approximately 80% of my rides were either in this category, or people dependent upon the Essential Workers - patients, grocery workers, shoppers, Emergency Room drops and pick-ups, etc.

As well, in my community non-profit work, the movement of the homeless off the streets and into shelters, rehabs, and related facilities.

By the way, prior to the Covid-19 pandemic, the homeless, people seeking mental health services, and the underserved people in our communities were "slipping through the cracks."

During the pandemic, many of these people slipped right through the cracks to the very bottom. The deep pit of despair.

One positive element of driving during the pandemic is I obtained most of my real news from the doctors, nurses, staff, and many other frontline workers in the Hero category.

This was a welcomed sanity check that I could use to obtain a clearer perspective on the crisis from those who were daily in the middle of the fight.

Clinging on to every piece of information to help put the pieces together.

Then, as things began to get more under control with the virus, and back to normal, the love affair with our heroes went into a quick fade.

Well, just like our forgotten veterans, I will not forget the heroes of the pandemic. My list is a bit more generous to include our teachers, transporters, home health, nursing home staff, firefighters, paramedics, police, refuse collectors, and other dedicated people who keep the world turning.

Society's safety net.

Now, it seems that every day I have the privilege to continue thanking our heroes.

There are at least 10 rides each week where I can honestly tell the person, "Hey, despite what you no longer hear from the media and popular culture, you are still my hero. Thank you for all you do. I understand your work is more than a job. It's a calling!"

Forever in debt.

***

"Where have all the Heroes Gone?
Short Time Passing
Where have all the Heroes Gone?
Short Time Ago"

Yes, of course, I'm exercising a little artistic license in borrowing from the iconic work of folk legend Pete Seeger, and his song "Where Have All the Flowers Gone."

Sorry, Mr. Seeger. I couldn't resist.

I'm encouraged that so many servant-hearted people in our society are being recognized as the true heroes they are and have always been.

Sadly, I also realize our predictable human condition.

Daily, as I drive across the region, I cannot help but notice large, colorful billboards and banners praising these saints of society.

I predict these banners, signs, and sentiments across the country will fade as quickly as the Covid sun rose on our planet.

I trust some will remember.

Always essential!

***

As noted earlier, this was written during the Covid-19 Pandemic and the gushing love affair with our essential workers and heroes by the media and popular culture. Since that time, I must share that my easy prediction, based on historically proven human behavior and short-term corporate memory, was sadly, right on target.

How easily we forget and sometimes, returning to normal is not always what it's cracked up to be.

Just ask our forgotten, and most surely essential, heroes.

Dialysis

Any person who has ever driven on a rideshare platform has likely spent time with people who were outpatients of some type. These rides occur almost every week. Going to and from hospitals and rehab facilities with walkers, wheelchairs, canes, oxygen masks, tanks, and other devices.

And people going to and from dialysis centers.

The stories from all these individuals are wide and varied. People from all walks of life, backgrounds, cultures, and ages.

One person who was going to kidney dialysis three times per week shared his story which I would like to share with you.

I accepted the ride on the rideshare app and drove to pick up my passenger. When I arrived, I saw a very thin man walking from his house to the car. He was walking slowly, with deliberate steps, assisted with the help of a walker which held his bag of dialysis equipment. His walk was more of a shuffle, and he was seemingly exhausted by the time he reached the curb.

I got out of the car to greet him.

We worked together to get him into the back seat, and I placed his walker in the trunk.

He was breathing heavily.

We immediately connected and began our conversation as we headed toward one of the local dialysis centers.

In a raspy tone of voice, he began sharing details of his long, hard journey.

He disclosed his anger about his family, financial situation, and, of course, his medical condition. Ultimately, he began partly blaming himself for his current condition.

Mostly, I listened and empathized with him.

Six years prior, he had his first kidney removed. Two years ago, he had his second kidney removed, and received a kidney transplant. His life situation was further complicated when he lost his job and insurance at some point between the first and second kidney removal.

He explained he was simply unable to afford the $400 for his kidney rejection medicine, so he discontinued taking the necessary medication. As a result, his second kidney was ultimately rejected and removed two weeks prior to our meeting.

Currently, he has no kidneys, and he is totally dependent on dialysis to live.

When we arrived at the center, I got out of the car, retrieved his walker, and helped him out of the back seat. He was extremely thankful and appreciated both the ride and the opportunity to openly vent during our trip together.

I thanked him for a great conversation. We blessed each other, hugged, and smiled.

I then got back in the car and watched him slowly shuffle into the dialysis center. He was determined to continue the good fight.

I was deeply touched by his story and took a moment to reflect on our ride as I watched him enter the door. I jotted some notes in my ride journal and headed for the next story.

Life goes on, and I am constantly inspired by humankind, and the will to survive. Seeing brave souls suffer through overwhelming adversity.

The human spirit is something to behold.

Mean-Spirited, Critical Complainers & Poor Attitudes

I suppose all the above could simply be summarized under the header Mean-Spirited, however, I believe that there are many motivations and underlying reasons for a variety of negative human behaviors. These three can be seen regularly, combined or independently, in the rideshare world. Not to say I'm somehow excusing negative behaviors, but honestly recognizing my own shortcomings, especially under pressure or severely fatigued, I must give others a bit-o-grace.

In life, and especially in this line of work, to work with a wide range of people, one must go through the process of gaining a balanced perspective regarding the human condition. All the conditions noted in the above header are commonplace events, so the sooner one manages this reality, the better.

By the way, the understanding and management of human attitudes and conditions applies to both drivers and riders in the rideshare world.

Here are a few thoughts to illustrate my point:

1. First off, the problem, or mistaken response, could be me.

   I could be misinterpreting a comment, gesture, facial expression, silence, tone of voice, etc. wrongly.

   As a fellow human being, I bring my history into the rideshare experience, for better or worse, and one resulting part of that equation is expectation.

   My expectation, or perhaps better put, preference, is that people should behave with a common sense of decency and civility towards fellow humans.

   This is a result of my upbringing and experiences growing up. It is also my desire to act this way towards others, albeit I fall short at times.

   Of course, I understand my desire for common courtesy and basic manners may be seen by some as somewhat of a naive kind of mindset, or quite old-school, in this age of hatred, distrust, strife, and division amplified by our popular culture and global media every minute of every day.

Frankly, I don't completely buy into much of this distorted portrayal of humankind. I see it as a divide-and-conquer agenda in many cases.

In my experience, and in my viewpoint, the extreme portrayal of "bad" human behavior does not represent the global majority.

I have a tested and proven reasoning that most people are simply on their personal life journey. Each trying to figure out their way in life, learning how to love, live well, work, enjoy their cultural and religious communities, or simply survive as best they can.

I say, proven reasoning, because six-plus decades of living and learning about myself and fellow humans, have taught me so. First-hand research, so to speak, and reinforced by knowledge of human history.

As well, the complementing experience of 25,000 plus rides over the past seven years, and spending precious time with so many people, is also factored into this conclusion.

We may focus our attention, and even have an appetite for the worse depictions of human nature, but these negative focus points are not representative of most people on this planet.

2. The person getting into my car could be going through an extremely difficult day or, as I like to say, "season, "in their personal life.

   Stress, fatigue, illness, addiction challenges, relational issues, workplace drama, motion sickness, fears, financial concerns, school finals, death of a loved one, and lest I forget, global pandemics, all play a part in behavior.

   You name it. The list is long and varied. We are all impacted directly or indirectly by these realities.

   To put it another way, life in this world can greatly affect our attitudes, one way or another. It's how we, as people, are wired.

3. Cultural norms and nuances, country of origin, and language differences can also contribute to misinterpretation of behavior.
   What may come across as a demanding or condescending tone of voice, may simply be the way people normally speak to one another in other cultures.
   What may seem like bad manners, may simply be different from Western Cultural expectations of what is often considered to be good or bad manners.
   What may come across as disengagement or aloofness, may simply be a language barrier or shyness.
   Patience, understanding, and a willingness to set aside the quick judgment of the situation, can help make the ride a good experience for all.

Now, with all the above being said, and at the risk of overtly displaying what might be interpreted as me being a professional enabler of bad or wrong behavior, let me assure you that there are those who are intentionally Mean-Spirited, Critical, Complainers and People with Poor Attitudes.

For some twisted reason, it's who they are, it's an important part of their identity, and they relish in the "sweet spot" of their questionable behavior.

Perhaps it's a control issue of some sort. Who knows.

So, regardless of the sphere or universe in which you operate, you will undoubtedly encounter people who seem to delight in being a so-called hater.

Fortunately, based on my experience, they are in the great minority.

I would have to emphasize that the intentionally Mean-Spirited Person is in the Top Ten list for Worst Rideshare Experiences Ever.

Let me share one story with you in this regard.

I was driving in Washington D.C., and I picked up a well-dressed young man.

I would guess he was in his early thirties.

Before he closed the car door, he began yelling at me, "Why are you sitting there like a stupid B****, let's get this F****** S*** on the road dude! "

Now, I know what some of you are thinking at this point, kick the S.O.B out of your car.

Well, this ride was in the days prior to the Covid-19 pandemic. Before some of the top rideshare companies began to take driver concerns more seriously. Granted, in any profit-driven organization, there is a natural tendency to favor the person who pays the bills, i.e., the riders.

At the time, with an abundance of available drivers, coupled with high attrition or turnover, the rideshare companies often took rider complaints quite seriously, and rightly so, but often at the expense of many drivers who were removed from the rideshare platform for days before the complaint was researched and ultimately resolved.

Although I've heard hundreds of such stories from rideshare drivers who were adversely, and arguably unfairly impacted by the methodology, I contend that it's part of the cost of doing business as an Independent Contractor.

However, over time, through listening, negotiation, and a sincere desire to find a good "balance" in managing complaints from both drivers and riders, these companies developed and strengthened their policy standards hoping to achieve fairness.

The work in achieving this fairness goal continues to this day.

Sorry for the brief digression folks. If you knew me well, you would understand I enjoy a short side trail now and then in my conversations.

So, back to my story.

The first thought that ran through my head was this guy is having an awful day.

Maybe he just got fired, or had a terrible meeting, or, or, or.........

Then, the rapid-fire critical and abusive spirit permeated the entirety of my vehicle.

"Hey B****, apparently you don't understand English, get your A** moving!"

"I'm running late and it's your F****** fault! You're a F****** idiot! "

At that point, I "justified" his behavior based on his concern about running late. I deduced that this may be the reason for the abusive language and nastiness.

As the minutes passed, I came to realize this was just a part of his unique personality.

"Do a U-Turn now!"

I responded, "I can't. It's illegal. "

In a sarcastic tone of voice, he said, "It's illegal. It's illegal. You're a sorry A** P**** who doesn't know how to drive and I'm making sure (Rideshare Company Name) knows about your F***** up driving. "

I made the U-Turn.

"See A******, that wasn't so bad. Now, speed things up and get through that light before I call (Rideshare Company Name) and report your A**. "

I obeyed and exceeded the speed limit.

Note: If a rider reports a driver for Unsafe Driving, or for a bad attitude, etc., as this person was threatening, the rideshare company, out of an abundance of concern for safety, will remove the driver from the rideshare platform (App) until the complaint is investigated as mentioned earlier.

Some riders know this fact well and use it to their fullest advantage to exert control.

"Can't you drive any faster?"

"You're the worst (Rideshare Company Name) driver I've ever had in my life. A sorry excuse of a person. A real Piece-of-S***! "

He was smiling from ear to ear in the backseat.

The guy was really enjoying his ride.

He had me just where he wanted me.

Before I allowed this person to ruin my day, and find myself in emotional escalation, I did some self-talk.

First off, I only have 8 more minutes with this person in my car.

He may report me to complete his abusiveness, but I have no control over what he chooses to do.

If (Rideshare Company Name) removes me from the App due to his complaint, so be it.

I have no control over what the company decides to do in this case.

I can rate him at the end of the ride and ensure that I'm never matched with him again.

This mind re-alignment through a little self-talk, and prayer, helped my perspective during the remainder of the ride.

His abuse continued.

I was more at peace.

He left the car, clearly angry that I did not engage in his drama.

His parting word was not "Thank-You. It was "P****! "

Well, this P**** did not get a complaint registered with the rideshare company.

And further, this P**** will never be matched with this rider again.

I gave him a One out of Five Rider Rating on the App.

Zero is not a Rating Option.

Yes, I'm smiling!

Falling Through the Cracks

As I've noted previously, there are stories in this book that are inspired by both my rideshare work and my support in the community non-profit world.

Due to legal, ethical, and proprietary medical reasons, I cannot detail specific ride stories. I can tell you is most of the non-profit clients fall into the category of "You Think You've Got It Bad?"

In short, I just want to take a moment to highlight the men and women living on the street, in tents, and in homeless shelters. People who are often not seen and easily discarded by our society. Members of our human family. Disowned, disrespected, and considered a nuisance by many.

Marginalized and desperate for help.

There are many reasons why these individuals, and in some cases, families, find themselves in such sad, and often dangerous, situations. Some are self-inflicted issues due to addictions and criminal history. Others are due to divorce, domestic violence, the deaths of caretakers, and illness. Some are due to job loss or lack of education. Some people are from other countries and unable to speak English. They have difficulty finding work and navigating the system.

The above is a short list.

There are so many reasons and so many complications which result in their current state.

Many of you have heard the expression "slipping through the cracks." This phrase is often used to describe a person or situation that simply dropped off the radar screen.

In the case of the homeless and marginalized populations across our country, when Covid-19 and the global pandemic swept across our country, many of these people "fell through the cracks."

No slipping. It was a dramatic and severe free fall.

The system was overwhelmed, or unable to respond effectively. Access was extremely difficult. Shelters became a moving target as populations were impacted by the virus infection. Hotels were converted into temporary shelters. Hospital emergency rooms were flooded daily with people seeking help.

In my travels, I was equipped with masks, some money, water, and food to hand out to people on the street corners. I'm so thankful for friends who helped to find and secure face masks for me to continue this effort.

Meetings and conversations I have with people on the street begin with the way I greet most people. Hello, how are you doing, what's your name? Sometimes this is tough from your car on a street corner, but I attempt to make the effort when possible.

It's a simple act, but it speaks volumes by breathing a little life and dignity into them.

They matter, and their name matters.

Yesterday I was driving in the city, and I saw a man which prompted me to sit down later in the evening to begin writing this story.

He was in a wheelchair at a traffic light. This situation is not very conducive to making it easy for people to hand him something from their vehicle. The man looked very drawn and sickly. Frail. He was holding the all-too-familiar cardboard sign with black lettering. However, in his case, I was taken by the words on his sign.

"I'm Not a Monster."

I was deeply touched by this human cry expressed on his little placard. There are so many ways to offer commentary on this event, but here's what it stirred in me at the time.

In Mary Shelly's 1818 classic novel, Frankenstein, it was never quite clear who the monster was in the story. Many believe the creature, which was assembled from human cadaver parts and brought to life by the scientist, Dr. Frankenstein, was the monster. Still, others believe that Dr. Frankenstein himself was the monster. His laboratory experiment, which got totally out of hand once the creature came to life, was completely Frankenstein's fault. The creature, or creation if you will, simply fell into the situation through no choice of its own. The resulting havoc and fear in the community ultimately tagged the creature as the monster.

Complicated and debatable for certain, but I believe the scenario is pertinent to the cry from the poor soul in his wheelchair.

Who, or what, is the creator? Who is the monster?

During the months of the global Covid-19 pandemic, I wrote a song titled, Falling Through the Cracks, to describe what was happening to the homeless and marginalized population.

Here are the lyrics:

Falling Through the Cracks by Bob Reilly
Broken Systems
Broken Spirits
Broken Bodies
Broken Dreams
Faceless People
All around us
Far too often
Never seen
Falling Through the Cracks
Falling Through the Cracks
Falling Through the Cracks
Falling Through the Cracks
They're the ones
That some call vagabonds
As so many turn their backs
But they're the ones
Who God loves perfectly
Falling Through the Cracks
Falling Through the Cracks
Falling Through the Cracks
Falling Through the Cracks

Postscript: Less than a month after I saw this guy with the sign, I caught him out of the corner of my eye. Same intersection. This time, I drove around the block, hit an ATM, and walked to where he was erratically, and dangerously, wheeling himself in the middle of the road between a line of cars sitting at the traffic light. When the light changed, he nearly got clipped as he frantically moved towards the curb.

Once he was on the sidewalk I approached him, introduced myself, and asked his name. We had a little light banter and I inquired why he wasn't using his "I Am Not a Monster" sign. He told me what I suspected. The sign made him feel even worse about himself. It was too much on top of the people passing by with judgmental stares. He felt he was buying into their cruel labeling. He was their monster, and he was beginning to accept their categorization. I shared my Frankenstein story with him, and he began to get very emotional. He fully understood my point on the creator and monster question.

In fact, he knew the story all too well on a very personal level.

I asked if we could pray together. Then, I slipped him some cash.

I walked back to my car with many thoughts swirling in my head.

No easy answers.

Spice of Life

Back in the 1980s, I wrote a light jazz instrumental song called "Spice of Life."

I heard the phrase, variety is the spice of life, when I was younger, and I really embraced the idea. At the time, I was exploring new, spicy world cuisines, so it added sensorial weight to the concept.

Variety is the spice of life and became one of my life mantras.

The reason I'm sitting here at my laptop, in the middle of Winter, banging out this book at 3:58 am, is another one of my life mantras.

Completion.

Although many projects tend to overlap in life, my goal, especially when tackling big projects, is completion. Hence, one positive result of this self-commitment is narrowing the scope of juggling projects. I have become much more selective in which projects are critical, life-enhancing, necessary, and important enough to take on and finish.

Both variety and completion play an important role in my rideshare adventure.

One of the things I've found so endearing, and in some ways addicting, about the rideshare journey is the random, unpredictable experiences offered by the very nature of the service.

As the famous philosopher, Forrest Gump, once said, "rideshare is like a box of chocolates. You never know what you're going to get."

Or something to that effect.

Think about it.

Over the past seven years and over 25,000 rides, I would often take notes on the types of rides I would manage over the course of a typical day.

For example, notes from a typical day might look something like this:

15 rides on a Tuesday.

High school teacher
Health care worker
Intern on Capitol Hill
(2) university students

Microbiologist
Pediatric Nurse
Mother off to work and dropping (2) children at daycare
Emergency room pick-up (cancer patient)
Crossing Guard
Local media celebrity heading to an evening D.C. fundraiser
"Plugged in" Electrician
Happy Stoner
Baseball fan heading to the stadium
Grocery store shopper with groceries to load in the trunk

My marketing tag for "Rideshare by Robert," has been and remains, "Every Ride's a Short Story, "and they are.

Variety.

Every age group, every tribe, every nation, every altered state. every self-identifying possibility has likely spent time with me on their rideshare journey.

As I like to say, I've spent time with many fellow humans, moving through space and time in my vehicle, and I've been honored to share a small slice of their lives in the process.

I have learned much, and I've grown in many unexpected ways as a person.

I believe all parties have benefited from the time well spent.

If variety is the spice of your life, then maybe a rideshare trip is worth a ride.

I will do my part to complete the trip safely and enjoyably.

Lastly, I will close out this essay with one more of my life mantras.

Keep moving!

Covid Memories: Trudy

The following story was written during the Covid-19 Global Pandemic. It was one of the writings I journaled during the virus pandemic crisis under the header Diary of a Hugger During the Covid-19 Crisis.

***

The Covid-19 Global Pandemic has been revealing so many memories, fears, emotions, and insecurities in people's lives.

Daily, I hear the cry from my back seat, sometimes openly and loudly, of people's hearts.

Often, we pray together. Sometimes, we cry together. Sharing our deepest thoughts and common humanity.

Our fragility.

I will share one such personal memory triggered by our Covid-19 Pandemic living.

Weeks before my mother, Trudy, passed away on July 18th, 2012, we sang together at her nursing home in Maryland. As a little boy, I remember her singing around the house. I was captivated. I believe she was the earliest instrument God used to stir my spirit to sing.

I'm so thankful that I have been able to continue using God's gift of music and create new songs throughout most of my life. I have participated in live music presentations both inside and outside the church.

A photo of my mother in the nursing home popped up on my Facebook timeline this morning. The photo triggered my memory. I know it wasn't an accident. During these times, in which most of the deaths from the virus are our treasured elders across the globe I can't help but consider God's purpose in this crisis.

Over the years I've pondered the question of God's purpose in so many things that happen and seem counter to a God of love and mercy. Over and over the question of purpose. I must admit, I still don't fully understand. I usually chalk it up as a great mystery and move on. And yet, God has allowed all types of natural disasters and events to speak to humankind throughout history.

Please don't ignore this possibility.

This is a global event, touching every corner of the planet earth. All tribes and nations.

Just as in the days of Noah, people went about their normal lives, buying, selling, marrying, loving, and hating, until the big event.

If you're able, please put aside your resistance for a moment to believe such things and entertain the possibility that a creator God is speaking to us through the natural world. For now, let's assume that Covid-19 is not a man-made virus, as some have speculated.

My question to you is this:

If there is a God of the universe, what do you believe God may be saying to the entire world these days?

I can tell you first-hand, that the back-seat responses from riders to this question have been amazing and enlightening. I've learned a lot from the responses. As well, the responses are as varied as the riders I transport every day.

Worth pondering.

Ironic Twist

Another chilly February morning in the city. Another day of driving, or mining, if you prefer, in search of diamonds, gold, and precious gems.

Stories.

I found one, as usual, in an unlikely and surprisingly inspiring circumstance.

Amazing how the mysterious gift of creation works, eh?

The seeds of creation and inspiration are everywhere.

I accepted a ride request and headed to the pick-up location. I arrived at an apartment complex and two young men came out laughing, playfully punching one another, and yelling loudly. This animated behavior continued as they climbed into my car.

"Hey, guys! Hope your day is going well."

They either didn't hear, didn't care, or simply ignored my greeting.

I was invisible. No acknowledgment, no response.

We pulled away and headed toward their destination.

The pungent smell of weed, alcohol, sweat, and some unfamiliar chemical odor, quickly filled the car. They continued jokingly punching each other in the back seat as I overheard them graphically detail their sex acts with a woman they just shared back at the apartment.

Out of nowhere, one of the guys yells out to me, "hey, turn that racist s*** off!"

Then the other punches him and says, "man, that mother-f*****'s old."

I smiled.

I could sense a story unfolding and I was eager to see what was next.

Now, oddly enough, I'm not so easily offended by such obnoxious behavior at this point in my life. Perhaps after seeing similar situations regularly over many years, I've become numb, and maybe to some extent, I've normalized the behavior. Usually, I simply put it in the misbegotten follies, ignorance, and foolishness of the youth category.

And, in some cases, I can easily forgive such behavior based on the context of their lives in our culture. I believe many young people are a result of failed systems, whether it be familial, school, or social. Some would argue, bad behavior is bad behavior and shouldn't be tolerated. Perhaps, but in the context of a short ride across the city, I am not going to belabor the issue.

You know, at some point, there's no use trying to reason with people who are presenting themselves as belligerent or mean-spirited, especially when on drugs, alcohol, or whatever.

What's the point?

I regularly converse and reason with people who are high on something, sometimes just themselves. So, it's not completely an issue of the intoxicant or drug.

It's an attitude thing.

Consider this:

In less than 15 seconds,

1. They implied I am racist based on the music I was playing.
2. They dissed me based on my age and appearance by making a derogatory statement.
3. You can draw your own conclusions about being called the MF word.

So, here's the ironic twist.

As it turns out, the background music I was playing in the car was from a local classical music station. And, to further the irony, the radio station was celebrating Black History Month and highlighted Black composers from around the world.

The station had just played a stunning symphony by a remarkable composer.

Florence Price.

I call her remarkable not only for the inspiring music she composed but also for the fact that she was the first African American woman to have her work performed in 1933.

Florence was born in 1887 and died in 1953.

Florence was born less than 25 years after slavery ended in the United States.

I can only imagine the adversity she faced as a Black woman in the late 1800s, and throughout her life, here in America. Yet, she knew her calling and tenaciously persevered in her craft.

And we are all better for it.

My personal favorite is her Symphony #1 in E minor. She poured out her soul into this piece. The imagery it evokes in my spirit takes me on a sweet journey of the mind.

And so, I accommodated these young dudes, turned off the Florence Price music, and listened to their playlist, complete with numerous F-Bombs, N-Words, and highly descriptive sexual content which some argue is sexist.

Welcome to rideshare folks.

In my humble opinion, people will still be listening to Florence Price's compositions in 100 years, and perhaps not the composer of the blasting audio composition playing in my car.

I believe people, across the globe, will still be inspired by her life, her achievements, and her works long after this moment in our history passes.

I could be completely wrong.

Only time will tell.

Story Headers

I thought sharing some of the story headers and content that didn't make it into this book might be fun. As a matter of fact, there are some stories that didn't even make it to the list below. In sharing this with you, it reveals part of my thought process as I was outlining the plan for writing my book. The headers, or story names and categories, were already in my journals in many cases. Many were in my heart and mind. And still, a few of the headers unfolded as my writing adventure was underway.

I like having these candidate stories in my pocket as I continue to write. They are also excellent fodder for my planned Rideshare by Robert podcasting, and YouTube Channel episodes.

Here's a handful of headers I hope you enjoy.

Let your imagination go wild!

- A Common Humanity
- Pet Lovers
- BPF (Best Phlegm's Forever)
- Do as I Spell, Not as I Yell
- Fellow Artists
- Backseat Confessions
- Weapons and Other Toys
- Flashers, Flaunters, and Freaks
- Gone Fishing
- Holy Day Identity Crisis
- Science Non-Fiction
- Grumbling to Humbling
- Homeland Heartbreak
- Ice Breakers
- I'm Gonna F*** You Up
- Keep It Up America
- Diary of a Hugger During the Covid-19 Global Pandemic
- Liberia
- Mask Art

- Names
- PDA Rides
- Perspective
- Rider Snapshots
- Roberto Bandito
- Rocking N' Riding
- Talking Trash
- Musical Serenades
- Storm Tracker
- The Anime and Comic Universe
- The D.C. Lawyer Who Hates People
- The Invisible Driver
- African Marriage Proposals
- The Martians Got It Right
- The Server
- Tribalism
- Unusual Circumstances
- What Are the Odds?
- Recurring Rides
- Military & Government Contractors
- Let's Ride
- Hacking, Coughing, Sneezing & Drooling
- Categories & Types
- Grunters, Ear Budders & Phone Talkers
- Kids, Students & Young Adults
- Newbies
- Evangelists
- Hipper & Hopper
- The Science of Art
- Growing in the Box
- Como E?
- Final Mile
- Matchmaker, Matchmaker
- Dope
- Sunday Preacher

- First Day
- Car Concerts
- Allergies
- Silence can be Golden
- Consulting
- Fairway to Heaven
- Nodding Off
- African Marriage Proposals
- The M Thing
- Front Stage
- Sights and Sounds
- Packed House
- Service Animals, Emotional Support Pets, and The Exotic
- Episodes Are Only a State-of-Mind
- Social Science
- Flick Offs and Road Rage
- The Potomac Hood Illusion
- Celebrities, Political Leaders, and Media Types
- Tolerance, Patience, and Grace
- Where's The Auto-Tune?

Keep posted.

You'll never know the rest of the story until you know the rest of the story.

For The Love of God

The following essay was written during the Covid-19 Global Pandemic in 2020. It refers to the many conversations related to the racial justice protests and riots across the country.

***

There's an old-school idiom, for the love of God. It was commonly used to express anger, frustration, or exasperation towards a situation.

Over time, like most popular culture references to God, the phrase has been watered-down quite a bit. For example, one modification is for the love of Pete.

For example:

"Fellow human beings, for the love of God (or Pete), please stop all this hating, racism, rioting, and killing of one another!"

I was sharing my heart this week with many rideshare clients about the subject of racism and reconciliation.

In short, most of the conversations centered on a common theme. That is, reconciliation and seeking peace vertically with God, move us towards reconciliation and peace horizontally with one another. Please excuse the up and down, side to side, word picture. Another way to express a similar point would be to seek God's peace internally and seek peace externally with one another.

Point is, seek God, seek peace. Or as you've probably seen on some bumper stickers, know God know peace. Same concept.

As you might expect, it would be worth noting that a great many people have significantly divergent viewpoints about God and the nature of God.

Some riders expressed the belief that the so-called, God-journey, is a personal inward focus. Change self, and thereby change the reality around self. Some prefer to refer to God with a small g. A handful of riders told me they believe each person is their god. Some describe their higher power. Anything bigger than self, so self can be put in proper perspective. And, yet others have determined that there is no such thing as a spiritual realm. Nothing is profoundly unique to humans in nature.

We are simply different creatures.

Humans are just another life form. We're born, and we die.

That's it.

Adios amigo.

However, I have found that most of the riders agreed that significant positive change can occur as one individual extends one loving act, one expression of kindness, or seeks to build a relationship and find common ground with another person.

Becoming other-focused. One life. One relationship at a time.

I would like to share some excerpts from several conversations, not to draw your attention to me, but rather to what I believe God has been doing in me and through me for many years.

My wife and I have been married for 37 years.

I am a father of three children of different races and countries. We began our international adoption journey in the mid-nineties.

My children are now all in their twenties. My racial heart journey began long before my wife and I decide to travel to three countries to adopt and build our family. Frankly, my biggest struggle before our first adopted child was more about familial issues, not obstacles related to racial differences. I sought some counseling before adopting children to work through the questions when the children are not biological children. Both from the child's perspective and the parent's perspective. The very real racial and cultural elements were also brought into the conversation.

Here is what one counselor referred to as the familial setup.

I was one of nine children in my family. I was named Robert Edward Reilly Jr. Through some wise counseling, I worked through the common issues of generational expectations in adoption, and I was able to move forward with God's plan to build our family.

When our children were babies and toddlers, I used to read, pray, and sing songs with them before bedtime, including one popular song that goes, " Jesus loves the little children, All the children of the world. Red and yellow, black, and white, are precious in his sight. Jesus loves the little children of the world."

A simple message in a simple lullaby-like song.

Not anything like the nightmare-producing prayer many people my age might remember hearing as a child.

"Now I lay me down to sleep. I pray to the Lord, that my soul to keep. If I should die before I awake. I pray the Lord, my soul to take."

"Wahhhh!"

"I don't want to go to sleep mommy. I'm scared. "

Maybe even scarred, for that matter!

Horror movie stuff.

Over the past seven years, God has placed me in a unique box to serve people in unique ways. I have found a deep purpose in my role.

My car is a unique box. A vehicle, if you will, for God's purpose.

Serving, in the truest sense of the word.

I have spent time with people from many tribes and nations, from across the planet, right here in the Mid-Atlantic region.

Building quick relationships, having deep conversations, encouraging one another, sharing, celebrating, laughing, crying, singing, loving, learning, and being.

In short, living.

Over 25,000 rides and counting.

Many stories. Many lessons. Many lives.

In closing, I will share one story from yesterday which may help illustrate how God is using me, in small ways, every day, to help heal racial relationships.

In the middle of a raging thunderstorm and tornado warning, I picked up an elderly Black woman outside a Maryland grocery store. She was hunched over with a cane, leaning on a cart filled with groceries. Her daughter, who arranged the ride, called me before the pick-up and asked if I would give her mother a helping hand. I arrived at the store. I helped her mother into the car and loaded her groceries in my trunk. We were both soaked by the torrential rain from head to toe. Her little umbrella was a useless tool as the rain and wind blew in a sideways manner.

Upon arriving at her apartment, I helped her out of the car and brought her and her groceries to the 3rd floor. She was very appreciative. We prayed together and in so doing, we blessed each other before my departure.

Simply amazing!

This woman reminded me of my mother in her advancing years.

Hunched over, walking slowly, a hint of uncertainty in her eyes and need of support.

As well, the concerned daughter, asking for special care for her mother, reminded me of my own six sisters who would have done the same thing for our mother.

One story, one encounter, one act of kindness, one blessing, one life at a time will surely help to heal the racial divide.

As they say, good people, pay it forward.

***

In closing this essay, I would like to add an important word to the conversation.

R-E-S-P-E-C-T.

When my children were young, I coached soccer for five years. Respect was the first word on the list of goals for my team each season. Self-respect, the opposing team, referees, and spectators. The word, win, was the second word on my list. Some parents pulled their kids off my roster because they wanted the word, WIN, in bold letters, at the top of the list. They didn't even want a list.

Only the one word, WIN.

Well, we didn't win every game, but we lost with dignity and good sportsmanship.

Respect.

We did win several championships along the way. That was certainly sweet, however, something far greater was happening. Our teams were united under a banner of respect. Something that will carry these young people further in life than a great headshot or left foot kick into the goal.

I say all this to ask each of you to apply respect to all people on their life journey.

Respect for their physical, emotional, and spiritual being.

If you tackle this undertaking well and keep your head down, you'll be hitting the goal consistently.

Practice makes perfect, and I can assure you that every day will present far more opportunities than you can ever imagine practicing your skills.

And guess what, in your pursuit of respecting yourself and others, you will win more than you lose.

Guaranteed.

I'm Sorry

Sometimes that's all that can be said.

I recently had an early morning weekend ride. I picked up the young person, said hello (by name), and asked how her morning was going.

She said, "terrible! "

I told her, "I'm sorry and I hope your day goes better."

She was immediately on her phone. She had the phone on speaker so I could overhear the entire conversation.

"Hello, this is (name) from (towing company). How can I help you? "

She explained that she had been in an accident the night before and her car was towed.

Bad news.

When she asked where the tow yard was located, he told her it was approximately 25 miles from where she lived. Easily an hour away.

Bad news.

She inquired if her insurance company could recover her vehicle and drop it closer to where she lives.

He indicated they were closed on the weekend and would open again on Monday at 8 am.

Bad news.

I could hear the tension in her voice and the escalating frustration.

She then asked if the insurance company could move the vehicle first thing on Monday.

He said yes, but she would need to sign a required release document.

Bad news.

In a response, which included a few expletives, she asked him to send over the release documents and she could do a digital sign-off for approval.

He told her this wasn't possible. She had to come to the tow yard and physically sign the release documents.

At that point, she went off.

Take cover people. Incoming!

I guess you might say, technically, I was experiencing a form of road rage.

The F-Bombs were exploding. The S-Missiles were flying. My little car was in a battle zone.

She threw the phone down and sobbed.

The remaining 5 minutes of the ride were silent.

When we arrived at her destination, I told her that I was so sorry for her car situation and hoped everything worked out.

She thanked me and walked away, head bowed, wiping the tears from her eyes.

I closed out the ride on the app, lifted a silent prayer for her, and headed toward my next adventure.

Funkenstein

One of the amazing things about the creative energy flowing out of the rideshare experience is the inevitable domino effect. That is, once you enter one door, or universe, a whole new world of inspiration unfolds.

Such is the case with the song I wrote entitled Funkenstein.

Some of you may be familiar with the popular Country song "It's Five O'clock Somewhere." It's an Alan Jackson, Jimmy Buffett collaboration with the basic theme that, somewhere around the world, the time is Five O'clock pm, and therefore, it's happy hour time.

Well, there's some truth in the song.

Pretty much everywhere on the planet, there's a celebration of some sort going on 24/7.

Over the past six years as a professional designated driver, I've been right in the middle of many celebratory events.

Sometimes the lines become blurred between when the spirit of celebration ends, and the ride begins. However, that's another story for another day.

I would suggest keeping your dark glasses nearby. Never know when they will be needed.

As a result of my unique vantage point, and role, I've been invited to quite a few celebration events on this journey. Private and public parties, BBQs, concerts, etc. It's nice to know you are deeply loved and appreciated during the ride.

Or, at least until the riders' buzz wears off!

Anyway, this convergence of driving, engaging in fun conversation, and a part-time attitude inspired the song, Funkenstein. Yes, to answer your potentially inquiring mind, Funkenstein is a fictitious place but could be anywhere in the world.

As a side note, there is a fun shout-out in the song to my friend Johnny Castle, an outstanding local musician (bass), vocalist, songwriter, teacher, and inspiration to many. He has performed all over the world. Johnny shared the stage and met many well-known people and bands in the music business. Jimi Hendrix, Rod Stewart, BB King, Steve Miller Band, NRBQ, and The Byrds, to name a few. If you don't have tears in your eyes from side-splitting laughter or heartbreak listening to Johnny share his stories from the road, you better check your pulse!

Also, I referenced one very well-known root blues group, Mark Wenners' band, The Nighthawks. One of the many bands Johnny C performed in and traveled with over the years. Mark Wenner and crew certainly have their own spicy stories and celebrity moments under their hats, and behind their harmonica's, for sure!

The lyrics to the song are below:

Funkenstein by Bob Reilly

There's a party down in Funkenstein
Everybody's catching a ride
Got an invitation
Think I'm gonna drop on by
Join the celebration
Whatever it may be
Take a look around
And what's there to see

Party down in Funkenstein
Everybody's catching a ride

Party Down in Funkenstein
Everybody's ready to roll
Music and some DJs
Guaranteed to put on a show
The scene is truly rocking
Songs that we all know
People on the dance floor
Yelling, "Go, Go, Go! "

Party down in Funkenstein
Everybody's ready to roll

Lil' Sheeba Martin
is wearing a bright red hat
Johnny C, the Nighthawk,
is wondering where it's at
Did he leave it in his rideshare?
Underneath the seat?
Better bet that when he finds it
things will sure be sweet

Party down in Funkenstein
Everybody's feeling all right

There's a party down in Funkenstein
Everybody's saying goodbye
I'm the designated
driver for the rest of the night
Get 'em all home safely
Tuck 'em all in bed
You can disregard the thing that I just said!

Party down in Funkenstein
Everybody's catching a ride

This song, and several other originals, were written with lyrics and music. They are being recorded for an album of songs inspired by stories from the Rideshare by Robert book and the rideshare experience in general. The songs will be available on all your popular music streaming platforms.

Rideshare by Robert: Every Ride's a Short Song
Stay tuned!

Morning Mentoring Advice

Here's some mentoring advice I gave to a young rider who is just beginning her day and her songwriting journey.

The conversation took place during the Covid-19 pandemic.

She's hoping to make a living through songwriting. That is her dream. Below is the basic, heart-felt, advice I shared with her

I opened up about my long and winding road in the arts.

***

If it's your calling write music.

Use it if you've been given a special, healing gift for humanity.

I can tell you it's a very tough road to make as a songwriter. It's a tough job to make it as a musician. Especially during the global pandemic. Not just in the music business, but in the arts in general. If you're in the performing arts, life is not good right now. There is beginning to be some creative online content of live performances which may help keep the arts on life support.

Many writers, like myself, have been writing songs for many years because they're writers. Most learn there is little or no money in it, even if you end up performing, producing, promoting, and recording your original material as I have for over 50 years.

During our conversation, I asked her to consider live performance, social media exposure, collaboration, songwriting groups, building bands or partnering with bands, and advocacy support. That is, finding other people who can come alongside you on your songwriting journey.

I encouraged her to explore diverse and creative ways to get her songs heard. Nothing is off the table. Listen and learn from those who have succeeded and those who keep on keeping on.

Never give up!

Many times, during my career in the global supply chain logistics field, I considered setting my music aside. Life was extremely busy with the constant travel, marriage, raising three children, and just simply dealing with all the things life throws at a person.

Yet, despite the sometimes-overwhelming burdens of living, the music, live performance, recording, fellowship of like-minded music friends, and the joy of writing were my counterbalance.

The Ying to my Yang, or vice versa.

My self-healing therapy, and my healing therapy for others to enjoy.

I have had the good fortune of working with many gifted musician friends throughout my music career who love my original material. We incorporate several of my songs in every set of popular cover songs we do in our live performances.

I have also collaborated with fellow musicians and songwriters and performed mostly original material live at times. So, at least in paid live performances, I've recouped a small portion of my expenses along the way. Of course, you don't necessarily recoup the time invested. However, you are investing in something much bigger than yourself.

I told her that recently, I archived my older original collaboration songs on to SoundCloud.com. This is one avenue to promote your songs freely to the public. I gave her my locater on Soundcloud to check out my catalog of material- Bob Reilly Studio Originals & Coolaborations. I detailed how to get her music out on popular streaming platforms like Apple, Google Play, Spotify, and YouTube as I did with my most recent singles, and my albums, Work in Progress, Unexpected Ways, Perfect Love and The Journey Home. I shared my future goal of writing a book called Rideshare by Robert, and recording music inspired by stories in the book. I explained how she could access popular streaming platforms through third-party companies like DistroKid, CD Baby, TuneCore, and others.

Yes, promote, promote, promote. And, when you're done promoting, promote some more!

I encouraged her to align herself with a dedicated agent if she's devoted to this life pursuit. I suggested she should seek out mentors in the business to help guide her and encourage her along the way.

Believing in yourself must move from your mind into action. Thought life to application. Knowing your purpose and gifts and applying them is born out of such belief. Putting your ideas into action is the tangible evidence of the reality and strength of your belief.

Remember, if it's a calling, then it's who you are regardless of whether you make a lot of money through selling your songs or if you achieve great fame.

One of my often-used quotes is, "a good song is a good song." I laugh when friends echo this quote back to me at times. Usually, when we're practicing and preparing an original piece for live performance or recording.

If you write good songs, you can still move people and especially enjoy the magic of an idea evolving into a song performed for others to hear and enjoy. Also, don't minimize the joy and therapy which comes from the act of creating. That alone is worth the time and investment.

I explained to her that it's an amazing thing since I loaded material from the last 30 years onto SoundCloud and other social media platforms. There are now people from all over the world who have been enjoying songs they've never heard before from some relatively unknown songwriter in Maryland USA.

Pretty cool stuff.

I told her to enjoy the journey, enjoy writing good songs, develop her craft, and cherish knowing in her heart you are an artist.

Again, if it's who you are. Let the world know.

You are a songwriter!

Rev. Dr. Martin Luther King, Jr.

The essay below was written during the Covid-19 Global Pandemic. Passions were running high, and confusion, fear, and chaos reigned. And as human nature would have it, anytime something goes wrong, or can't be explained, people are quick to find scapegoats. Some persons or groups are to blame for the ills of society, and global pandemics are a trigger point as good as any.

Emotional and financial instability, uncertainty, lack of clear identity, and fear make for ready soil to plant distorted ideas and easy finger-pointing.

A perfect storm scenario for opportunists of every stripe, political belief, or otherwise to fill the void of normalcy.

Such was our global environment during this crisis.

Thereby solidifying the notion that chaos does indeed offer great opportunities for some.

During the dark Covid World, there was no more tolerance for moderate or middle-of-the-road politics. A person had to choose sides, and be all in. The very thick battle lines were drawn. The idea of collegiate or civil relationships with the other side was, and remains to this day, unacceptable to many. The very idea of negotiation was viewed as treasonous. This lack of civility, and hatred towards opposing parties, groups, sexes, races, and viewpoints, trickled down and out from our leaders into mainstream society.

The impact of this global, top-down poisoning will be felt for generations.

Politics was on the verge of becoming the blood sport it's often termed.

More like watching some contact sport than a time-honored tradition of a politician being a servant of the people. An extreme sport married with extreme theater.

So, here we are today.

My hope is for a more compassionate, and truly tolerant future for all people worldwide as I share this writing from our shared Covid history.

***

I almost committed myself to disengage from social media for a while and simply, let it be.

I can't.

I'm a writer.

I'm a seeker of the truth. I cannot sit silent. I will not apologize for who I am.

Every week, while driving in the city of Washington, D.C., I am reminded of Martin Luther King when I drive by his memorial statue off Independence Ave., or when I drive on Martin Luther King Ave. in Southeast. Then, of course, when we celebrate his life in January every year as a federal holiday.

In addition, I cannot count the number of riders who bring up Rev. King in their conversations. The current state-of-affairs, in our country and around the world, is heartbreaking. Vision and love are lacking among many leaders, and so, the life of Martin Luther King is further amplified as an iconic standout. He had both the gift of vision and love, and as a vessel of God's purpose, Rev. King marched forward, and his message was clear.

I completely understand why this current social-political movement disassociates from him and his call for peaceful protests.

To some, Dr. King was simply not radical, violent, or extreme enough to be considered a prominent figure in alignment with the *by any means necessary* mantra of today.

I believe they couldn't be further from the truth.

I just want you to know, that for me and many other people around the world, he helped to bridge some of the racial divides through his heart for all humanity. His non-violent heart for humanity. Rev. King was inspired by the non-violent protests model established by Mahatma Gandhi. He believed Gandhi took the love exemplified in Christianity and creatively forged the successful non-violent social-political movement in India.

Many considered the social change realized through Martin Luther King's inspired and bold approach to protesting was the 2nd civil war in the U.S.

His dream was our collective dream.

His life, unwavering faith, clarity, and his dedicated pursuit of truly non-violent protests exemplified self-control, grace, and undeniable maturity in a time when such constraint must have been unbearable for a Black man in this country. Through Jim Crow racism, God's spirit shouldered his burden and elevated him above the fray. His words and deeds, seasoned with determination and clarity, will inspire humankind long after the violence, hate, destruction, and the many isms associated with this present moment in history, pass on.

Thank you, Martin Luther King, for being a positive and desperately needed example of love and hope to and for all humankind.

Thank you for laying down your life in pursuit of your calling.

As an artist, I realize oftentimes stark contrasts bring out the beauty of a composition.

His social justice movement, and his very life, are a stark contrast to the current movement we see around the globe today.

I believe his own words summed up this concept brilliantly.

"Darkness cannot drive out darkness: only light can do that. Hate cannot drive out hate: only love can do that."

Rev. Dr. Martin Luther King's life was, and is, beautiful to behold.

The light of his life shines even more powerfully in the darkness of this present age.

Frenzied and Anxious

Among the varied challenges associated with the Covid-19 Global Pandemic was the 2020 directive that all students on F-1 and M-1 visas leave the U.S. and take their courses online. This created angst, uncertainty, and chaos among many.

One specific student from the Middle East made an indelible imprint on me during this confusing time.

I pulled up outside the U.S. Passport Office in the city, not too far from George Washington University.

The place was packed with young people.

I indicated on the rideshare app that I arrived.

Out of the group emerged an overtly anxious man in his early 20s.

He circled my car, opened one door, closed it, opened another door, left it open for around 30 seconds, and eventually climbed into the car.

"Oh s***, oh s***, oh s***!"

He was thrashing about in the back seat in what appeared to be a state of disbelief and shock.

"No, oh no, what can I do?"

"What can I do?"

I was at a loss for words. I wasn't sure what he could do, and he wasn't disclosing much except his concern for his student visa.

I asked if he reached out to his country's embassy or consulate.

It was as if I was speaking right through him.

He was in a daze and looking anxiously out of every window in the car.

"No, oh s****, no!"

We went about two blocks and he yelled for me to stop the car. I stopped the car, and he jumped out and ran down the street erratically.

The rear door was left open.

I got out of the car, closed the rear door, and climbed back into the car. I looked at his name on the rideshare app and closed out the ride.

A strange, disorienting sadness washed over me.

I turned off the app for several minutes. I took a deep breath, or perhaps it was fifteen deep breaths. I meditated on the moment and lifted a prayer for him.

I absorbed the experience in my mind and heart. Then, I turned on my driver app and headed for my next ride.

My next story.

The time with this young man was my shortest rideshare experience to date, and one I will not soon forget.

Full Circle

Earlier today, I had what I would call a full-circle experience.

I picked up a man outside a hotel in the city. He was heading to one of the memorials located on the National Mall in Washington, D.C.

The ride lasted about 15 minutes.

Almost immediately after getting in my car, we dove into a deep conversation about our lives. As I've disclosed throughout this book, I love getting deep. I would say, on most rides, my relational scuba gear is already on and I'm ready to explore what's beneath the surface.

I've discovered that mutual transparency is not only a gift to the rider in finding a safe zone to talk, but each conversation reveals and heals my own life as well.

All at no additional financial cost to either party. Only the cost of transparency.

Heal yes!

Within minutes of the ride, I discovered he was a priest in the Catholic church.

I told him about growing up in a family with eight siblings, attending Catholic elementary school, playing contemporary folk praise music at church as a teen, and how my mother would have been delighted if I entered the priesthood.

Well, Bob "Robert" Reilly may have been destined to become a man of the cloth if not for one major issue.

Girls.

I was more interested in chasing than in being chaste!

We discussed the scriptures, the global pandemic, our different spiritual paths, the furnace of marriage, and how God is always at work in our lives.

He shared his story about his upbringing, priesthood journey, loss of family, current life situation, and ultimately, some very significant personal challenges he was experiencing.

I sensed the extreme heaviness of his burden in his voice and spirit.

As we neared his destination, I pulled the car over and turned off the rideshare app. I asked if I could pray for him. He agreed, and we prayed.

His heaviness was noticeably lifted, and he was grateful. He left the car and said he would listen to my music album, keep posted on my book, and drop me a note when he returned home.

He thanked me for the ride and the prayer.

Before he closed the rear door, he leaned in and said, "you should become a Spiritual Director."

I laughed.

He smiled, closed the door, and walked away.

Well, I don't know about officializing, or putting a title to what God is doing in my life, however, I accepted his comment as a gift and considered it a beautiful compliment.

And a confirmation.

I entitled this story full circle because, during all the years on my spiritual journey, there's only been a handful of times when I've prayed with, and specifically for, a Catholic priest, one-on-one.

However, I've prayed with and for many other spiritual leaders, and people in general, on my life journey.

People of different faiths, beliefs, and denominations. I don't care where they're coming from or what they believe, or don't believe. Prayer is a gift.

I believe prayer is impactful, effective, and worth the time.

A conversation with the God of the universe.

I recall praying with a self-proclaimed atheist. This person was going through a lot of personal struggles and felt extremely defeated.

I asked if I could pray for him as we wrapped up the ride.

He said, "sure, it's a waste of time and energy, but you seem like a nice dude, so if it makes you feel better, go ahead."

I prayed, he gave me a whatever look, thanked me, and left.

Heaven only knows what happened after that.

So, when it comes to spiritual titles, I've always appreciated the title, fellow sojourner.

Open mind. Open heart. Seeking. Receiving. Sharing. Growing.

This keeps me open to so many fresh, and often, challenging views on beliefs and matters of faith.

A pastor friend of mine used to jokingly refer to his role as a professional holy man.

For paid spiritual leaders, I think this rings true.

The bottom line is that we are all works in progress regardless of title. Daily navigating this chapter of the eternal journey, we call life. It's no coincidence that the name of my most recent music album is called "Work in Progress."

All of us. You and me. All in process. All on a journey of discovery. Wild and wonderful at that.

I tell people all the time, that if you don't believe you're a work in progress, you have a lot of work to do. Nobody has arrived. Occasionally, when I have a conversation with someone about the idea of works in progress, I receive a retort such as, "I would argue some people are works in regress."

Well, we know that progress, in any shape or form, can sometimes look like two steps back and five steps forward. To one degree or another, and throughout our lives, regression is part of the human condition. Relax and keep moving forward. The obsessive pursuit of human perfection is an illusion, and in my estimation, a miserable undertaking if it dominates a person's life.

Works in progress.

Everything is part of our journey. All part of our story.

It is quite good to be fully alive.

A life imperfectly traveled, and perfectly blessed.

A New Beginning

Sometimes, the culmination of years, experiences, and the playing of many roles was designed for a particular purpose at a particular time in our relationships.

In most cases, we are simply being who we are, and don't fully realize our composite at the time. In a few cases, people will offer you a reminder of not only who you are, but where you've been.

Human mirrors.

The weather was cool as we were wrapping up another summer season on the East Coast. Funny how the reality of changing seasons was uncannily applicable to the ride I was about to encounter.

I picked up a woman at the airport. She waved me down as I pulled up and pulled curbside to assist in loading her luggage into the trunk. She climbed into the backseat, and we left the airport. Within 2 minutes of our departure, she began to sob uncontrollably.

I asked her if everything was okay. She responded with an apology and began to pour out her story.

She was born and raised in a mid-west city and married her high school sweetheart. Both she and her husband launched their professional careers after college. They had one child together. Things were hectic, but nothing outside the norm. In her mind, and by comparison with other couples, their life was right on course. She was optimistic and looking forward to the future, and perhaps another child. Her husband just got a promotion at work along with a very nice raise.

All was well. Until last month.

Her husband divulged that he was having an affair with another woman. He had no desire to continue with their marriage. He said he was no longer in love with her and asked for a divorce.

At this point in the conversation, she broke down again and I tried to console her as best I could. We both got very personal, deep, and transparent in our discussion. We both began sharing other stories about our lives. We laughed, we cried, and we healed a bit.

The ride lasted approximately 30 minutes.

When we arrived at her destination, I turned off the rideshare app. I got out of the car, opened her door, and popped the trunk to retrieve her bags. I told her that I would keep her, her family, and her situation in prayer.

She smiled and looked intently into my eyes. She told me that was the first time she was able to laugh in weeks. As she was chuckling, with tears in her eyes, she said I reminded her of her favorite uncle, priest, bartender, and counselor.

We both laughed.

We parted ways as she began a new season and a new beginning in her life.

I adjusted my hat of many colors for my next ride.

Smile

This morning I picked up a rider and for the sake of illustration, let's call him James.

When he entered my car, I welcomed him and told him he was the third James of the day.

He laughed.

I followed up by saying, "That's right, you are the third James of the day, but from what I can see, you are the best-looking and most intelligent of the bunch. "

He laughed again.

As we drove along, he told me we were heading to his chiropractor for an appointment.

I told him my chiropractor story.

"Yeah, was going to a chiropractor for a while for some spinal alignment issues. I was in a car accident about 15 years ago in Virginia. A person slammed into the side of my vehicle coming off an exit ramp onto 495. My car was completely totaled. So, I began seeing a chiropractor. The guy was hilarious. He cracked me up!"

I heard loud moans and laughter from the back seat.

Okay, so I fall into the category of bad dad jokes. I realize my humor can be eye-rolling sometimes, but my point is the third James of the day was relaxed and thoroughly enjoying the ride, therefore, I was thoroughly enjoying the ride as well.

Lots of smiles and laughter.

To see a fellow human being smile and hear a fellow human being laugh is both my mission and my reward.

2nd Chronicles 7:14

I extracted several of the stories in this book from one of my journaling projects entitled Diary of a Hugger During the Covid-19 Crisis.

During the darkest days and months of the pandemic, I continued to drive or to put it another way, I was driven. I was driven to not miss the opportunity to be close to others during the crisis. Driven to serve, in the true sense of the word. Then, as usually happens in life, blessings poured out became the blessing poured in. The mutual serving in the flood of emotions, hope, fear, encouragement, prayer, crying, laughing, and a greater appreciation of life.

Something deeply profound was happening. A fullness that I wouldn't and couldn't miss for the life of me.

It is not hyperbole to say total strangers became one as we faced this common, unseen enemy together. A global event, unlike anything I have seen in my lifetime.

2 Chronicles 7:14 can be found in the Hebrew Bible or the Christian Old Testament. These words were written approximately 2,400 years ago. During the most intensive days and nights of the Global Pandemic of 2020, I meditated on these words of promise and healing. Boy, how we needed healing on so many levels. I worked closely in support of the front-line, whom the popular culture then referred to as essential workers. The people, seldom recognized, whom society relies on every day for their care and services.

God spoke to me through the ancient scripture, and I shared the ancient words with as many as were open to receiving. Believe me, people were clinging to anything for hope and truth as the world was reeling from the pandemics' impact.

People were encouraged, and the load was lightened by hearing the powerful healing promises. As well, a new song was birthed which I call 2nd Chronicles 7:14. The song was inspired by and based on the words in the scripture.

On many rides, people asked me to sing the song which I did joyfully.

I never want to forget the lessons in this season. The melody and words of the song reinforced my resolve and my purpose during the pandemic. They are embedded in my heart and mind.

Here are the lyrics to the song:

2nd Chronicles 7:14 by Bob Reilly

If my people, who are called by my name
Will humble themselves and pray
Seek my face and turn away
From all their wicked ways
Then, I will hear from heaven
I'll forgive
And heal their land

Father, hear our cry
As so many die
Heal this world that you created, and you love
Draw the broken near
Dry their every tear
Send your angels with your mercy from above

If my people
If my people
If my people

Special Thanks

In closing, I would like to thank you, the reader of this book. I deeply appreciate your support and willingness to jump in and take the ride with me. If you enjoyed the experience, drop me a note, leave a review, and share Rideshare by Robert with others.

This book has truly been a community effort and so many gracious people contributed to the project.

First off, without the rideshare platforms, and the riders, there would be no book. My sincere thanks to the rideshare companies for your creativity and innovations in making this unique universe possible. My heart goes out to all the strangers, and friends, who physically shared time with me over the last seven years. My life is deeper and richer because of you, your life, and your stories.

To all my friends who climbed on board and made this book possible, I owe you a debt of gratitude I can never fully repay.

I offer sincere thsnks to the mentoring of new friends globally from different literary groups offering generous advice. For input from fellow writers and dear friends, including Cynthia Lynn, Tony Glaros, Mark Opsasnick, Ev Foster, Ellen Berrahmoun, and Jon Paul, my heart is so appreciative. For the popping gold tire Rideshare by Robert logo design, special thanks to Paul Goldbeck. For the whimsical "Mo Peace Sign" driver sketch, I give thanks to my longtime friend, Art Allen. For the wonderful comments and reviews from friends in music and media, thank you to Cerphe Colwell, Susan Colwell, Joe Goulait, Johnny Castle, and Steven Rosch.

Thanks to my publisher team, BookLocker, and the gifted Angela Hoy for her knowledge, guidance, patience, and love for writers.

A deep debt of gratitude goes out to my family, immediate and extended.

The generations who came before and the ones to follow.

Abundant thanks to my three children and especially my wife of 37 years, Pam, for going on this journey with me. In particular, the last ten months. The gestation period in growing my little book baby. Pam transitioned from questioning me every day about why I was up between 3:30-4:00 am, to "what time is it? Oh, you must be working on the book."

I love you, and now you can roll over and go back to sleep.

Until the next book.

About The Author

Bob Reilly was born in Washington, D.C., and currently resides in Maryland. This is Bob's first published book, with several creative projects in the works. These would include recording original songs inspired by stories in the book, and a YouTube Channel with an audio Podcast. All under the Rideshare by Robert brand.

He is a prolific songwriter, recording, and performance artist. You can find his latest albums and singles on your popular music streaming platforms.

Bob Reilly: Work in Progress
Bob Reilly: The Bridge/Unexpected Ways
Bob Reilly: Perfect Love
Bob Reilly: The Journey Home

More about the author can be found in the Forward section of this book.

www.weinotproductions.com
www.ridesharebyrobert.com
info@weinotproductions.com

Facebook:
Bob Reilly
Bob Reilly / Weinot Productions
Rideshare by Robert
Bob Reilly & Joe Goulait Music/The Reilly Goulait Band

Instagram & Twitter:
#bobreillyweinotproductions
#ridesharebyrobert
#reillygoulaitband
#mopeaceliving

CPSIA information can be obtained
at www.ICGtesting.com
Printed in the USA
JSHW061218151122
33158JS00002B/6